Community of Life

IMAGINING
A NEW CHURCH

Building A
Community of Life

IMAGINING
A NEW CHURCH

Bill Huebsch

General Editor

ThomasMore®
– An RCL Company –
Allen, Texas

Acknowledgments

The Scripture quotations contained herein are from the *New Revised Standard Version Bible: Catholic Edition* copyright © 1993 and 1989 by the Division of Christian Education for the National Council of the Churches of Christ in the U.S.A. Used by permission. All rights reserved.

Front cover image, "Cross on Hill with Shadow" © Karlic Design, Baltimore.

Parts of "Imagine a New Church, Indeed!" by Bill Huebsch reprinted with permission from *Whole Community Catechesis in Plain English,* published by Twenty-Third Publications, P.O. Box 180, Mystic, CT 06355.

Send all inquiries to:
Thomas More® Publishing
An RCL Company
200 East Bethany Drive
Allen, Texas 75002-3804

Telephone: 800-264-0368 / 972-390-6400
Fax: 800-688-8356 / 972-390-6560

Visit us at: **www.thomasmore.com**
Customer Service E-mail: **cservice@rcl-enterprises.com**

Printed in the United States of America

Library of Congress Control Number:

7529   ISBN 0-88347-529-4

1 2 3 4 5   07 06 05 04 03

Contents

Preface

WHILE TRAVELING TO A MEETING several months ago, I listened to a fascinating radio conversation about the power and use of imagination in general education. I found myself intrigued about how the elements of that discussion might be applied to catechesis and its related ministries. By the time I arrived at my destination, I was convinced that a study of imagination and its applications would be an exciting way to develop the theme and program for the National Center's then upcoming thirty-first East Coast Conference for Religious Education.

Shortly after that trip, we were beset with stunning revelations of sexual misconduct and coverup that shattered the peace within our church and which eroded credibility and trust in our institution. It became clear that only facing these issues maturely in the light and confidence of the Spirit would restore the church's credibility and trust. It also became obvious that our conference program needed to expand to include how we might help deal with this critical situation.

So, with the help of our East Coast Conference advisory committee, we went to work developing a conference poised to do just that. With the theme *Imagining a New Church:*

Building a Community of Life, we offered folks a gathering that would envision ways of restoring trust in the church while offering them practical resources for enriching their ministry.

We invited conference participants, as we also invite you with this book, to imagine a church that has experienced a turnaround from its state of crisis and mistrust to a church with a life-giving framework that:

> Communicates a message that arouses confidence
> and trust,
> Captures the imagination of our culture and renews
> interest in its mission,
> Draws on our strongest energies to build
> God's reign, and
> Forms mature Christians energized
> to transform society!

Our committee felt that the key for guiding us in this period of reform is found in our myths and our images—for they hold up our values, beliefs, models, and sources of inspiration that unconsciously shape our attitudes and structures. They give us a frame of reference for our actions, for expressing our hopes, dreams, and fears.

We knew that, just as Jesus drew us into this metaphorical world of images and parables to break down old ways of understanding religion and God, we would need the full power of imagination to be open to the God who is being revealed to us today in reforming the life of our faith community.

With this book you'll discover how we explored this influential realm of myths and images at the conference. And you'll see how to imagine new, inspiring myths and images of participatory leadership, restoring trust and hope for our future.

It will also help you reclaim your God-given creativity, offering realistic ways of establishing environments that foster creativity and opportunities to nurture Christian imagination. You'll explore how imagination works. How you can develop and use it. And how you can draw on it to minister more effectively.

I'm delighted with the results of this book and most happy to be able to share with you so many of our conference's insights and suggestions. I want to thank Debra Hampton at Thomas More for all of her efforts in coordinating this effort, my old friend Bill Huebsch for bringing his many skills to bear on this work as general editor, all of the speakers/authors who contributed these wonderful articles, and our dedicated ECC advisory committee who shared their great wealth of wisdom in developing our conference program.

I hope that this book will contribute to the ongoing renewal of our church at this crucial time. I also hope that it will support and assist you in your ministry of building vital communities of life.

And finally, I hope it inspires you to *Let Your Imagination Soar!*

—Tim Ragan
National Center for Pastoral Leadership

East Coast Conference Advisory Committee:
Dennis Beeman, Director, Office of Christian Formation, Diocese of Richmond;
Anne Comeaux, Director, Office of Continuing Christian Education, Diocese of Galveston-Houston;
Jim Corr, Director, Office of Religious Formation, Archdiocese of Omaha;

Jim DeBoy, Vice President for Mission, Bon Secours
Baltimore Health System;
Jeanne Schrempf, Director, Office of Evangelization and
Catechesis, Diocese of Albany;
Maureen Shaughnessy, S.C., Assistant Secretary for
Catechesis and Leadership Formation, Department of
Education, USCCB

Introduction

"IMAGINATION," THE NOVELIST HENRY MILLER once wrote, "is the voice of daring. If there is anything Godlike about God it is that. He dared to imagine everything."

God dared to imagine everything. Imagination is the seed of hope, the first step to reform, the power that drives innovation, creativity, and faith. Out of God's great imagination tumbled all that we know, the whole of creation, and our very selves. God imagined each of us, one by one, head to toe.

In today's Church, possessed of a great vision and needed so badly in a world torn by violence, greed, and war, we must imagine the world as God does. We must imagine ourselves, our community, and our future as we believe God wants it.

This little book of essays by leading "futurists" in the Church is a powerful tool for you in doing just that.

Father Lou Cameli leads us off. He's the director of ongoing formation for the priests of the Archdiocese of Chicago, a renowned theologian, and a fine writer. His essay lays down the principles we must follow as we move forward together and imagine the future. "This new Church," he writes, "cannot be other than the Church that Jesus Christ gave us." This essay introduces us to a new understanding of "acedia." This insight alone will move you to a new level of imagination and hope!

The next essay is from the well-known author and professor, Tom Groome. Dr. Groome is on the faculty at Boston College but his greatest influence has certainly come from his important published works. In this essay, he draws from several of them to help us see how thoroughly *Catholic* it is to use our imaginations—for prayer, leadership, and even for church politics. This essay will lead you to the rest of Dr. Groome's work, and also to a renewed hope in what it means *to be Catholic*. His concluding remarks on Mary help you to see the fruits of imagination at work.

Next up is Father Anthony Gittins, C.S.Sp., a member of the faculty at the Catholic Theological Union of Chicago and a widely published author. In this remarkable essay, Father Gittins reintroduces us to Christ by retelling two of the stories about him from Mark's gospel. It's a compelling and almost mesmerizing approach to imagining our future because it brings us first back to our very roots in the life of Jesus. Now here we have reason to hope! Christ is still with us, as alive as ever!

We turn then to an important essay by Sister Maureen Shaughnessy, S.C., who serves as Assistant Secretary for Catechesis with the national bishops' conference in Washington, D.C. Sister Maureen's own love and devotion to adult formation as the norm of church life comes through loud and clear here as she imagines a new Church, filled with adults who know Christ and love the Church. This very practical essay is must reading for anyone who wants to develop adult formation at his or her own parish.

The next essay is a gem. Written by Diane Lampitt, Director of Catechetical Resources for RCL, it's a short retreat in itself. Read it slowly, putting down the book from time to time to allow her ideas to take up a permanent place in your heart and soul. There is no question that Diane will help you employ your own imagination to grow spiritually, to teach with more grace, and to really touch the lives of those around you. With the ease of a gifted teacher, Diane leads us through a reflection on imagination that itself fires our own imaginations. What a gift!

The next essay provides an honest and frank discussion of the roots of much of the recent pain the Church has been feeling: sex, sexuality, and human loving. No one is more qualified to write about this in a pastoral and loving tone than Father John Heagle and Sister Fran Ferder, F.S.P.A. This remarkable pair of church workers are codirectors of Therapy and Renewal Associates (TARA) in Seattle, Washington. Well-known authors and speakers, they give us an essay here that boldly challenges us with what is perhaps the greatest challenge for the Church today and in the future. "We cannot honestly imagine our future," they tell us in essence, "unless we become honest about sexuality, too." And they do become honest, with a tender and merciful language that is a model for the rest of us.

And finally, there is my own essay. It's really more of a poem, or a vision, written in free-verse form with whole community catechesis in mind. In a way, it draws all the previous essays into one big vision: a welcoming church, open, affirming and full of grace! It is, as Lou Cameli urged, a vision of the Church which Christ gave us. And in the words of Tom Groome, it rises out of the conviction that God comes looking for us! It stems from the stories of Jesus, as Tony Gittins tells them so well: "We can see! We need not go around spiritually blind anymore." With Maureen Shaughnessy, this essay calls us to welcome the adults of the church, to offer them a home again. And inspired by the words of Diane Lampitt, just let this vision arise around you; let it take its place within your own soul. And finally, this vision is the one spelled out with tenderness and passion by Fran Ferder and John Heagle as only they can do: This is, after all, about love.

The blueprint for the future of the Church is not like the blueprint you use when building a house. In the latter, every detail is spelled out with meticulous accuracy. Every inch is measured, every angle described. In the Church, though, we must imagine the future Church as God would. God's creativity unfolds around us, little by little. We can't predict beforehand how the terrain will be changed by an erupting volcano. We can't know for sure what creative urge will next amaze us with God's divine imagination!

This collection of essays helps us understand this. Little by little, we in the Church inch forward, going to God together, in the age-old Catholic spirit, empowered by the stories of Jesus, throughout our adult lives, steeped in imagination, and learning always how to love one another more perfectly. Imagine that!

Bill Huebsch

Contributors

Louis J. Cameli

LOUIS J. CAMELI is Director of Ongoing Formation for priests for the Archdiocese of Chicago, holds a doctorate in theology with a specialization in spirituality, and has served on the faculty of Mundelein University at St. Mary of the Lake, Mundelein, Illinois, as professor of spirituality, director of spiritual life, and dean of theology. He is the author of *Mary's Journey, Going to God Together, Ministerial Consciousness,* and *Stories of Paradise,* and coauthor of two volumes of the catechetical series *Faith First* (RCL) and theological consultant for the entire project.

Thomas H. Groome

THOMAS H. GROOME is Professor of Theology and Religious Education at Boston College, and Director of Boston College's Institute of Religious Education and Pastoral Ministry. He is the author of *Christian Religious Education,* widely regarded as the most important and influential contemporary work on the subject, and of *Sharing Faith,* a foundational work on Christian ministry, and most recently, *Educating for Life* and *What Makes us Catholic: Eight Gifts for Life.*

Diane Lampitt

DIANE LAMPITT is Director of Catechetical Resources for RCL–Resources for Christian Living, a catechetical leader, adult educator, and workshop facilitator. She holds an M.A. in religious education from Boston College and a certificate in spiritual direction. Diane has been a parish director of religious education, pastoral associate, and catechumenate director, as well as a diocesan director of evangelization, catechesis, and initiation for the Diocese of Charleston, South Carolina.

Anthony J. Gittins

ANTHONY J. GITTINS, C.S.Sp., is a social and theological anthropologist and a professor at Catholic Theological Union in Chicago with a wide range of experience in writing, teaching, and pastoral ministry in intercultural and international settings. His research focuses on the dynamics of inculturation by using anthropological and theological lenses. His pastoral outreach includes Chicago's disenfranchised, as well as cultures from Africa to the Pacific. He has authored several books, including his latest, *A Presence that Disturbs: A Call to Radical Discipleship.*

Maureen Shaughnessy

MAUREEN SHAUGHNESSY, S.C., former Assistant Secretary for Catechesis and Leadership Formation in the department of education at the United States Conference of Catholic Bishops, is presently General Superior of the Sisters of Charity of Saint Elizabeth. In addition to teaching at the elementary, secondary, college, university, and seminary levels, she has served as Secretary for Evangelization Education for the Diocese of Paterson, New Jersey and as General Secretary and General Councilor for her community.

Fran Ferder

FRAN FERDER, F.S.P.A., Ph.D., is Co-director with John Heagle of Therapy and Renewal Associates (TARA), a counseling and consultation center in Seattle. She is a licensed clinical psychologist, author, and nationally known speaker. She is a part-time faculty member in the School of Theology and Ministry at Seattle University. She has had more than twenty years of ministerial and professional experience as a college professor, psychological consultant for various religious communities and dioceses, and research director for a major social ministry study.

John Heagle

JOHN HEAGLE, M.A., J.C.L., is a certified mental health counselor, author, and nationally known speaker, and Co-director with Fran Ferder of Therapy and Renewal Associates (TARA) in Seattle. He is a part-time faculty member in the School of Theology and Ministry at Seattle University. John has more than thirty years of pastoral experience, including college teaching, campus ministry, justice and peace leadership, and ten years as a pastor. He is co-author with Fran Ferder of the recently published book *Tender Fires: The Spiritual Promise of Sexuality.*

Bill Huebsch

BILL HUEBSCH worked for five years each on the diocesan staff in Crookston and New Ulm in Minnesota and has served as vice president at RCL—Resources for Christian Living in Allen, Texas, and as an editorial advisor to Benziger. In 1990 he established the Vatican II Project to promote the spirit and energy of Vatican II. He has published nine books, including his *Vatican II in Plain English* series and *A Spirituality of Wholeness,* and was a contributor to *Continuing the Journey: Celebrating 40 Years of Vatican II.*

Louis J. Cameli

Building a Community of Life

Introduction

PERMIT ME TO BEGIN WITH A LITTLE AUTOBIO-
graphical note. I did my graduate studies in spirituality and
theology in the early 1970s at the Gregorian University in
Rome. It was a wonderful experience enhanced by the many
great and spiritual people I met in the course of my studies.
Among these was Mother Teresa. She came to the university
and spoke to us very simply, of course, but eloquently. She
advised us that if we wanted to be helpful in service to the
Gospel, we should not come to India. She suggested that we
stay home and care for the poor among us.

Afterward, there was a reception line and an opportunity
for each of us to meet Mother Teresa individually. I stood in
line wondering, "What am I going to say to Mother Teresa?"
I never really answered the question, and when the magic
moment arrived I just blurted out something that was maybe

the dumbest thing I ever said in my life. I said, "Mother Teresa, you're doing a great job."

When I stepped back from that encounter and my awkward words of affirmation and her gracious smiling acceptance of them, I began to realize something new about spirituality. So often spirituality has a very individual, personal cast about it. People think about *their own* journey, *their own* particular experience of God. I began to see spirituality in Mother Teresa more clearly and in a different way. I saw her as someone who obviously had a deep personal spirituality and a profound piety, but I also saw her making connections and bringing people together—the poor, the rich, her own community. She was raising the consciousness of the whole Church.

There were others like Mother Teresa visiting Rome in the 1970s—bishops from Africa, for example, who struggled *with their people* because of civil wars and violence and famine. These bishops witnessed a deep spirituality, an ecclesial spirituality, as they led their people together toward peace and toward God. And there were workers from Latin America—priests, religious women, and also lay volunteers—struggling for justice and for some dignity for their people. All of these men and women taught me to understand spirituality in a new and fresh way, that it is about more than just our individual journeys. In fact, we are truly going to God together.

The Second Vatican Council, which had finished several years earlier, also spoke of this larger sense of the spiritual life and spirituality. Several passages touched me deeply and continue to inspire me to this day. The first is from the very beginning of the *Dogmatic Constitution on the Church:* "Since the Church, in Christ, is in the nature of sacrament—a sign and instrument, that is, of communion with God and of unity among all men [and women] . . ." (1). In other words, the Church's identity is intimately linked to being an efficacious sign of the unity of God and all humanity—a rather extraordinary affirmation which I suspect we have not yet fully grasped.

Another passage from the same document definitively dispels the possibility of considering salvation or spirituality in a Catholic Christian context as an individualistic or private affair. It reads: "At all times and in every race, anyone who fears God and does what is right has been acceptable to him (cf. Acts 10:35). He has, however, willed to make men [and women] holy and save them, not as individuals without any bond or link between them, but rather to make them into a people who might acknowledge him and serve him in holiness" (9).

Finally, a passage from the *Pastoral Constitution on the Church in the Modern World* offers this remarkable, perhaps even startling picture of our life together in the Church: "Furthermore, the Lord Jesus, when praying to the Father 'that they may all be one . . . even as we are one' (Jn. 17:21–22), has opened up new horizons closed to human reason by implying that there is a certain parallel between the union existing among the divine persons and the union of the sons [and daughters] of God in truth and love" (24). This is a vision of spirituality unlike what we encounter in the popular culture. There is nothing here about personal enhancement, good vibrations, and basking in my own karma. The spiritual vision of the council and, indeed, of our most deeply grounded traditions has to do with being part of a people going to God together.

In the contemporary American context, this collective and communal sense of spirituality is very challenging. Think of Robert Putnam's recent book *Bowling Alone: The Collapse and Revival of American Community* (Touchstone Books, 2001). Both Putnam and the earlier work of Robert Bellah (*Habits of the Heart,* University of California Press, 1996) help us to understand how much we prize individualism in our culture, sometimes in such a way that it has made us deeply lonely. American Catholics are immersed in that culture which prizes individualism, and they can be compromised by it. At the same time, in our American Catholic Church experience, there have been some salient reminders that we do go to God together.

Think of African-American Catholics who have struggled together. They stayed, and now they sing and pray, "We've come this far by faith." Note that it is "We" not "I." Think, too, of some of our new Asian immigrants, particularly Filipinos and Vietnamese, and their celebrations and devotions that bring people together in the Church. Of course, our Hispanic-Catholic populations, with their sense of *familia*, of *un pueblo en marcha*, a people on the move, underscore the communal nature of our spiritual journey.

These are extraordinary reminders to all of us that we are going to God together. Still, despite this wonderful and often countercultural spiritual vision, opened up by the Second Vatican Council and witnessed in different ways in the Church, we have trouble. Clearly, in the Church we have trouble. These are difficult times. Although it is scant consolation, it is not just the Church but almost every institution of public life that does not seem to deliver what it ought to deliver. In the Catholic Church, however, we are affected in a particular way. Although we have a beautiful vision of going to God together, we know that we stumble, that we have our difficulties. We now face problems which are of a magnitude scarcely imaginable a decade ago. So we turn to the theme of imagining a new Church.

We think of a new Church; we try to imagine a new Church, a renewed Church. There are currents of distress and dreaming, and in this flow there is perhaps some confusion about the sense of a "new or renewed Church." What exactly does this mean? What does it look like?

Imagining a "New Church"—What It Cannot Be

First of all, we ought to eliminate any misunderstandings that might arise when we talk about imagining a "new" Church. We ought to note what it does not look like.

This new Church cannot be other than the Church that Jesus Christ gave us. It cannot have a different faith. It cannot have different sacraments. It cannot lose its apostolic ministry. Saint Paul, who never had a reputation for being politically correct, expressed it this way to the Galatians: "Even if we or an angel from heaven should proclaim to you a gospel contrary to what we proclaimed to you, let that one be accursed! As we have said before, so now I repeat, if anyone proclaims to you a gospel contrary to what you received, let that one be accursed" (Galatians 1:8). Paul is clear, and so must we be.

Someone gave me a Christmas gift last year, a copy of the new edition of the *Roman Martyrology*. (*Martyrologium romanum,* Vatican City, 2001). It has become a daily routine, a part of my spiritual practice now, to read the *Martyrology* each day. Each day, I encounter a list of the men and women, the boys and girls who across two thousand years all over the world gave their lives in witness to the faith on that day. They shed their blood because they believed. This daily spiritual practice has, first of all, helped me to put my own problems in context. Also important, indeed, even more important, is the realization that faith is precious. Fidelity, adhering to that faith, is of paramount importance. We cannot just let go of the gift of faith that the Lord has given to us.

Imagine a new Church, but not a church other than the one Church Jesus Christ gave us. We cannot create it by the dint of our own efforts, and we cannot make it in our own image and likeness. Wherever this imagination takes us, it must stay faithful. At the same time, a renewed Church must be a renewed Church, not just patched up, not just with a few cosmetic touches, to make it look a little bit better. The Church is in service to the emergence of the reign of God in this world. Jesus talked about the reign of God in very dynamic terms—of the growth of seeds and plants and leaven. The Church is meant to be alive. Renewal means renewal. I am drawn to the words of Blessed John XXIII at the beginning of the Second Vatican Council. He warned people that the Church is not a museum. It is neither a place housing antiquities, nor is it a preservation society. The Church remains faithful to Tradition when it is dynamic, because Tradition itself is dynamic. In different places, Saint Paul speaks of the dynamism or movement of tradition using an old rabbinic formula, "For I handed on to you, what I myself received. . ." (see 1 Corinthians 11:23 and 15:3)."

There is dynamism and power in authentic renewal. So where does this leave us today? How can we imagine a new, a renewed Church? Permit me to share with you an analysis of the Church's situation today.

The Collective Temptation to *Acedia*

I believe that we in the Church are suffering from a collective temptation at this moment in our life together and in our history. This collective temptation assails us as we continue the renewal initiated by the Second Vatican Council. The council closed in 1965. For many people, the council is ancient history. It is finished, and whatever happened, happened. But, in fact, the renewal movement inaugurated by the Holy Spirit at Vatican II continues and probably will continue well beyond our time on earth.

We, the people of God, who are going to God together, are in a process of renewal. In the process, as I said above, we are suffering from a collective temptation. We are facing a temptation to *acedia*. This may be a new word and concept for you; allow me a word of explanation.

In the third and fourth and fifth centuries, there were men and women who felt called to a particularly radical way of living out the Gospel. These men and women felt deep passion and longing for the living God. They went out to the desert to find God, to be transformed, and to give themselves over in total loving surrender. This was the great and powerful spiritual and religious movement of the desert fathers and mothers.

When they were in the desert, barren and desolate as it was, they had a rich and challenging set of experiences. The desert is the place of radical solitude and self-discovery. It is also the place were God is found. Also lurking in the desert is the devil. Some of the desert fathers and mothers were astute and wise enough to mark down and to note for the rest of us the graces and the perils and challenges of their spiritual journeys.

From this period and from these writings, we have the seven capital sins which describe the inclinations, temptations, and patterns that lead to other sins and, ultimately, to the derailment of the entire spiritual journey. In my studies of the capital sins, one stands out as particularly menacing, both then and now. It is *acedia*, and it is the most dangerous capital sin because of its capacity to wreck a spiritual life in progress.

We translate *acedia* rather anemically as "sloth." We think of laziness and of those little animals at the zoo that hang on branches and do nothing all day. This is not *acedia*. It is much more complicated. The word comes from the Greek *akadeo*, which means "I don't care." *Acedia* was also called the noonday devil because this temptation would come to those people who had embarked on a special and intense religious journey to God and had been on the journey for a while.

The temptation of *acedia* manifests itself in three different ways. First, a voice might come to the desert solitary and say, "Well, so you've been out here in the desert, haven't you? You've been reading the Bible carefully, attaching yourself to the Word of God. And you've been praying and fasting and denying yourself sleep. But take a look at yourself. You really haven't changed all that much. Read your own heart. Not all that much has happened. Why don't you just go back home? Why don't you go back to where you were before?" This is the first form of the temptation of *acedia*—"Go back! It hasn't been worth it."

The second form of this temptation also assails a person who has been on the journey for a while. Again, there is a voice. "You came out here and did a number of very good things and God is pleased with you, but, really, you probably could do a lot better if you did something else. Why don't you go visit the other hermits or organize a new program? You could advance spiritually a lot faster doing something different." The second form of the temptation is "Do something else."

The third form of the temptation again occurs after the person has been engaged in the spiritual journey for some time. A similar voice speaks. "Oh, you've come out here to this wasteland. You wanted to be attached to God with all your mind and heart and soul. You wanted to surrender yourself in love, but look at you. You're still a small-minded, self-centered, selfish person. Nothing will ever work for you to change you. Why don't you just collapse in your own sadness? You might as well just be depressed." The third form of the temptation is "paralyzing sadness."

Here, then, is the triple form of the very insidious temptation of *acedia:* Go back, do something else, collapse in your own sadness.

Now, think about the Church today. The Church has been consciously and deliberately involved in renewal for over forty years—from the beginnings of the Second Vatican Council. We have been on this intentional journey together, a journey that is a quest for God and for our transformation. We have been on the journey for a while, and now this triple temptation afflicts us. We must face it and address it together.

The first form of the temptation tells us to look at the good things that have happened but then to focus intently on negativity—the confusion, the inadequate catechetics, the bad liturgy, the failure to work for social and societal transformation. The devil says, "Look at the mess. Why don't you go back to the way the Church was before the Council? Let's have restoration." The second form of the temptation again invites us to see some good but to wonder how much better it would be if we did something else, something entirely different. "Let's just forget about the Church as we've known it. Let's radicalize it and construct a whole new thing." The third form of the temptation also touches us individually and collectively. "Look at the present moment of the Church—the difficulties, the confusion, the daily crises chronicled in the newspapers—and all this after years of struggling for renewal. It looks hopeless. Why don't we just stop and collapse in our sadness?"

Now, this kind of collective temptation to *acedia* is not new. The very same temptation plagued the people of Israel in Exodus, moving from slavery through the desert to the Promised Land. The story is familiar. People have been liberated by God. And then they are in the desert. After a while they begin to wonder, "How are we going to eat, how are we going to drink, will we ever arrive in this 'promised land?' Maybe we should go back to Egypt. We know it was slavery, but we knew the work, and we had food, and there was water." The first form of the temptation is to go back.

Again, the people of Israel are in the desert. They walk, they wander, they stumble, and they wonder. "Couldn't this go faster? Couldn't there be a better way, better than God's way? Maybe we should try something different. Let's build a golden calf." The second form of the temptation is to do something different.

Finally, the third form of the temptation manifests itself. "We're not going anywhere. We just keep going in circles. We might as well just sit down here in this desert and die." The third form of the temptation is to embrace a paralyzing sadness.

The pattern of a collective temptation for people who are on a spiritual journey together is not new. It is, I believe, the major and most dangerous temptation affecting us in the Church today. Go back, do something different, or collapse in sadness.

This triple temptation we face is truly a temptation to halt the conciliar renewal which Pope John Paul II has called the great blessing of the twentieth century (*Novo millennio ineunte*, 58). I would also suggest that it is a failure of holy imagination. We cannot imagine the new, so we are drawn to restore something that we think existed. We cannot imagine a renewed faithfulness, so we are drawn to radicalize the Church and build something according to our own image and likeness. We cannot imagine at all, and so we move toward depression.

I am suggesting a path for confronting this temptation, a way of moving beyond *acedia* in its triple form. Fundamentally, successful confrontation of *acedia* means that we fire up holy imagination so that we can continue on the journey to God together in a renewed way. One important way to do this is to look at men and women of our tradition who have lived and experienced not our precise situation but situations which have some parallels to our own. How did they stir their imaginations for living in the Church? They did so by way of retrieval and response. They retrieved the Tradition and the Word of God. They retrieved the experience of other holy men and women who had gone before them. At the same time, they were future-directed. They were fully committed to responding to their particular situation and then moving forward. Of course, this double process of retrieval and response entailed risks, but the risks were necessary to fire their holy imagination. I will offer some examples to illustrate what I mean. Perhaps these examples will suggest ways for you to think about our life in the Church today.

Saint Benedict and Saint Scholastica

Think of Benedict and his sister Scholastica. They lived between A.D. 480 and 550. Do you have a sense of those years? Perhaps not. They were years of dramatic social destabilization. Roman society with all its flaws and failures provided an orderly context for life. But in those years, that order fell away. Barbarians invaded. Life became uncertain. The Church was profoundly affected. What does Benedict do?

Benedict retrieves the second chapter of the Acts of the Apostles. "They devoted themselves to the apostles' teaching and fellowship, to the breaking of bread and the prayers. . . . All who believed were together and had all things in common" (Acts 2:42, 44). He retrieves an image and a spirit of community. Benedict and Scholastica retrieve that holy memory embedded in the life of the Church and respond by creating new forms of community. Of course, they founded monasteries for monks and nuns, but these monasteries became vital spiritual centers for everyone. They were communities that could provide stability and hope to people who lived in an unstable world.

Saint Francis of Assisi

Think of Francis. He lived in a situation much different than that of Benedict and Scholastica. Francis' world and the Church were not destabilized; they were perhaps too stable. The Church for Francis was present and structured and organized and perhaps even comfortable. In this context, Francis retrieves a dimension of the Word of God, something deeply imbedded in the life of the Church. He retrieves the end of Mark's gospel: "Go into all the world and proclaim the good news to the whole creation" (Mark 16:15).

In the Church of his time, a Church grown settled, Francis imagines a new way to give mobility to the gospel, to give the gospel feet, to go out and proclaim it in very particular ways. He brings to the forefront, for example, the blessed humanity of Jesus and a deeply personal love of the Savior. In Francis' time, theology—faith seeking understanding—had become the domain of universities, and in the process it had become very abstract. Francis gave the gospel specificity and mobility by drawing us back to the Incarnate Word. This is holy imagination in action.

Julian of Norwich

Think of Julian of Norwich. (See *Julian of Norwich Showings,* Paulist Press, 1988.) She is an extraordinary woman of our tradition. She is famous in many circles because of her expansive sense of God as both father and mother. She lived in the fourteenth century. If you really want to understand Julian of Norwich and her context, read Barbara Tuchman's book, *A Distant Mirror* (Ballantine Books, 1987), which details life in the fourteenth century.

In 1373, Julian experienced a series of visions, deep contemplative experiences that fed her and enabled her to feed the Church. She lived in an extraordinary moment—the time of plague. This was a terrible time when about twenty million people, one third of Europe, died. Perhaps there are some places now in Africa where the AIDS epidemic is raging, where there might be a parallel situation. For Julian's contemporaries, however, there was the additional burden of ignorance, because this was a time before we understood infectious diseases.

The plague caused terrible social upheaval. It was a medical disaster. It was also a spiritual disaster that shook and challenged the faith of believers, for the plague engendered great anxiety and a deep sense of guilt and dread. "Is God against us? Are we at a time like that of Noah and the flood, when God was set to wipe out humanity?" These were the questions believers raised. Julian retrieves a very significant part of our tradition about prayer, such as we find in Paul's letter to the Romans: ". . . for we do not know how to pray as we ought, but that very Spirit intercedes with sighs too deep for words" (Romans 8:26). Julian couples her prayer experiences with another teaching in that same chapter: "We know that all things work together for good for those who love God, who are called according to his purpose" (Romans 8:28).

From her contemplative imagination, Julian is able to frame a pastoral response. She imagines a way of encouraging the Church and believers to move forward, to keep going. It is summed up in her extraordinary words: "All will be well, all will be well, all manner of things will be well."

Saint Therese of Lisieux

Think of Therese of Lisieux. (See her autobiography, *Story of a Soul,* ICS Publications, 1999.) She lived at the end of the nineteenth century in a church environment tinged by Jansenism. This incorrect and incomplete spiritual mindset focused on following the law, almost to the point of trying to earn one's salvation, although no one would quite say it that way. Spirituality in Therese's environment was fundamentally joyless. Holiness seemed limited to those dramatic instances of people who had great mystical visions or who practiced heroic mortification and self-denial.

In this daunting spiritual situation, Therese, a rather revolutionary young woman, retrieves the beatitudes of the Gospel and the sense of spiritual childhood. She re-imagines spirituality in a life of simplicity, her "Little Way," that is a spiritual path of engaging daily life and a deepened commitment and love within the very circumstances and situations in which we find ourselves.

This is a revolutionary approach to spirituality and holiness that is democratic or accessible to everyone. It is involved and sustained in daily commitment, and love, not law, is the great integrator. Therese shows us an exercise of holy imagination in a Church situation that seemed, to a great extent, to be frozen. She retrieved and responded, and has made a powerful difference for many, many people.

Franz Jaegerstaetter

The last name I mention is not as familiar as the others. I hope that he becomes better known. This is Franz Jaegerstaetter. In the early sixties, Gordon Zahn published a remarkable book about Jaegerstaetter entitled *In Solitary Witness: The Life and Death of Franz Jaegerstaetter.* (Templegate Publishers, 1986). Franz Jaegerstaetter's story is one of the most remarkable to come out of the Second World War. Here is a brief summary of his life. He was born in 1907 in St. Radegund, a small village in upper Austria. His natural father was killed in World War I. Later, he was adopted by the man his mother married. In his youth, Franz had gained a reputation for being a wild fellow but in general his daily life was like that of most Austrian peasants. He was not a terribly educated person, just basically literate. He was a farmer, doing the regular and humble work of farming.

In 1936 he married a girl from a nearby village and they went to Rome on their honeymoon. A Catholic by birth, he experienced a religious awakening, apparently about the time of his marriage, and then later served as sexton of his parish church. When Hitler's troops moved into Austria in 1938, Jaegerstaetter was the only man in his village to vote against the *Anschluss*. Although he was not involved in any political organization, he did undergo one brief period of military training. He remained openly anti-Nazi and publicly declared he would not fight in Hitler's army.

After many delays, Jaegerstaetter was called to active duty in February, 1943. By this time he had three daughters, the eldest not quite six. He maintained his position against fighting for the Third Reich and was imprisoned first at Linz and then at Berlin. After a military trial, he was beheaded on August 9, 1943 (See *In Solitary Witness*, p. 3). At every step, he was discouraged from maintaining his stance against the Nazis and against fighting in the German army. Even officials of the military tribunal made him offers and wanted to cut deals, for example, to have him serve in a noncombatant position as a medic. Priests with whom he consulted and even his own bishop discouraged him from persevering in his decision. They told him that he was not morally obliged to hold fast to the position that he had assumed. They counseled him to consider the good of his wife and three daughters and suggested that he could licitly make some accommodation. Jaegerstaetter, however, had retrieved a deeply embedded part of the tradition. It is evident in Matthew 10:28: "Do not fear those who kill the body but cannot kill the soul; rather fear him who can destroy both soul and body in hell." And he had retrieved something from John's gospel: "In the world you face persecution. But take courage; I have conquered the world!" (John 16:33).

In a remarkable way, in a seemingly compromised ecclesial situation, Jaegerstaetter re-imagined a new integrity, a new way of holding fast, of resisting, and, at the same time, affirming the coming of the reign of God and God's sovereignty in human affairs.

Conclusion

I believe that we in the Church today share a vision: We are going to God together. This vision is grounded in the Word of God and in our Tradition. Still, when we view our situation today in the Church and in the world, it is easy for us to succumb to that triple temptation of *acedia* individually and collectively. We hear the voices: "Go back. Do something entirely different. Just collapse in your sadness." But this temptation must be resisted. This temptation is a radical failure of holy imagination. When we look back on the holy men and women who have gone before us, we begin to get some clues about our response for today. We learn to retrieve from the Word of God, to retrieve from the lives of those who have gone before us, and we learn never to forget to respond, to look ahead, and to move into our future in God. Pray that we will have the courage and strength to do just this.

For Reflection

⬧ With whom do you "go to God"? Who are the companions that most assist you in your spiritual journey?

⬧ How does your parish help its members "go to God together"? What opportunities do you offer people who wish to share the journey?

⬧ Think about the town or neighborhood in which you live. What needs are there which your parish can address? Who is overlooked or rejected? Who is in greatest need?

Letting Imagination Soar

WHAT MAKES US CATHOLIC? POSING THIS QUES-
tion while urging that we "let imagination soar" might
surprise you at first. The social scientists tell us that identity is
an owned sense of the continuities that mark our lives; our
identity reflects what is stable and continuous over time. So
we might not think of claiming identity as the way to let imagination soar. Identity would seem more an exercise for
memory than for imagination.

But this is only because our enlightenment mentality has
too easily separated the functions of mind—reason, memory,
and imagination—as if they are separate faculties. In fact,
René Descartes (d. 1650) prized the triumph of mind alone,
to the diminishment of the other two. By contrast, I believe,
Saint Augustine (d. 430) had it right. Writing some 1,600
years ago, he proposed that reason, memory, and imagination
should work together as closely as the three Persons of the

Blessed Trinity—in other words, distinct and yet functioning as one. Further, imagination depends precisely on the memory for its images. Remembering well is the key to imagining creatively. This is true of us as persons, and of the church as a community of faith as well.

To Memory for Imagination

The proposal that underlies my presentation, then, is that we must return to the deep structures of our Catholic Christian tradition so that we may allow our imaginations to soar. And surely, we're badly in need of the hope and new life that imagination can lend at this point in time. Even if it was the best of times—we know that it isn't, but even if it was—"What makes us Catholic?" would still be a great question to ask.

So, what about this great tradition of faith that distinguishes us even within the body of Christ? Of course, we are first and foremost Christians; let us always begin there. We hold in common with all our Orthodox, Anglican, and Protestant brothers and sisters a deep faith in Jesus Christ as the Messiah and liberator of history. We believe he was the Son of God who showed us how to live within God's reign, and now, through the Spirit, he empowers the whole Christian community to carry on God's work of salvation in the world. As the Second Vatican Council reminded us with urgency, baptism makes all Christians members of the one Body of Christ, the Church in the world. Our attempts to name our particularity as *Catholic* Christians must never threaten but should enhance our bond with all Christians. Yet there is surely something distinctive about our identity as Catholic Christians. How do we name what makes us particular? How do we reclaim it and refurbish it in these times? How can we approach this rich tradition, go to the communal memory, in ways that will prompt our imaginations to soar— toward hope, new life, and, indeed, Church reform?

There is a fascinating book that just appeared from Twenty-Third Publications, *Vatican II: Forty Personal Stories*. It's a lovely book with contributions from eminent, prominent, distinguished famous people, like Avery Cardinal Dulles and Abbess Joan Chittister, Richard McBrien, and Monika Hellwig. It's fascinating to read what has happened to them since Vatican II. I was reflecting on this the other day after having the privilege of receiving Eucharist, because I noticed that everyone present went up to receive communion at the 12:00 noon Sunday Mass. Now reflect on this. How many of us remember the time when the only people who received Holy Communion did so at the early Mass on Sunday morning, at the 7:00 A.M., the 7:30, maybe the 8:00 Mass? At the later Masses, not too many people would receive because they wanted to have their breakfast and they had to fast from midnight. Think about the symbol of the reception of Eucharist in our lives and all that has happened. A handful of devout people would go to communion on a Sunday. The church actually required people to fulfill their Easter obligation, to go to Eucharist at least once a year.

On October 11, 2002, we celebrated forty years since the opening of Vatican II. Posing the question, "What Makes us Catholic?" should bring us back to the council's great unfinished agenda; there is still much to be done in order to realize its promise. Perhaps one blessing from the terrible scandal of child abuse by clergy and its coverup by their superiors which we've experienced will be to shake us out of complacency and return us to the council's program of *aggiornamento*—renewal of the whole Church. Though much has been accomplished, I believe "we've only just begun" to function as a Vatican II church.

At this time we surely need to reclaim that baptism entitles every Christian to participate in the governance and oversight of the Church. We know that God, in God's great mercy, is capable of drawing good from evil; surely to return us to our rights and responsibilities for the Church conferred by baptism will be such a blessing arising out of the recent scandals. "In the one Spirit we were all baptized into one body," wrote Paul (1 Corinthians 12:13), and we must realize that in this Church no one is any more baptized than anyone else. The dreadful scandal of recent years should awaken us from our slumbers to realize that baptism forbids Christians a laissez-faire attitude about their church—precisely because we love our Catholic faith, and cherish it for the ways it is so life-giving for ourselves, and for the world.

Even these brief reflections on baptism make the point that the best hope we have at this time, the best way to let the imagination soar so that we can renew and reform the Church, is to return to the deep structures of the tradition, to the core convictions that make us Catholic Christians. I'm thinking of the life-giving streams of meaning and faith, of purpose and commitment, of holiness and justice that form the great river of Catholicism and have been running through this great tradition for the past two thousand years. These fresh-flowing waters, the deepest rather than facile memories, nourish new life and encourage imagination to soar.

I overheard an argument between two women, two friends of mine—one totally opposed and one totally in favor of women's ordination to priesthood. The argument went back and forth, and eventually they turned to me and asked me what I thought. I said to them: "What amazes me is that there's profound disagreement between you about this very important, crucial sacramental issue that goes to the very core of our identity as Catholic Christians. What also amazes me is that there's so much common ground between the two of you—deep structures upon which you agree."

They said, "Tom, you haven't been listening."

I said, "Yes, I have. You both care deeply about the whole sacramental economy of our tradition. You both care deeply about Eucharist and that people have ready access to quality celebration of Eucharist without driving a hundred miles or waiting a month. You're both deeply committed to the sacrament of holy orders, that it is a valid sacrament, that it's worth fighting about. You're not even questioning the validity of the sacrament. You're claiming it and then arguing about who may participate therein." And I named five or six great doctrines of our faith that were the common ground on which both of these women agreed.

When we go to the treasury of tradition, let us remember the wisdom of Jesus. As he advised, the scribe who is learned in the reign of God is like the head of a household who takes from the storeroom both the new and the old (see Matthew 13:52). Jesus knew well the correlation between memory and imagination. We should never go to the tradition just to find something to repeat one more time. As Wolfhart Pannenberg warned, the surest way to kill a tradition is to cling to it as a museum piece, to try simply to repeat it. We go to the tradition in order to find the images that will prompt our imaginations to soar.

Parenthetically, let me raise a caveat before proceeding, a caution that we must ever keep before us in claiming any religious identity. We need to move cautiously because religion has been used—tragically—to turn people against each other, to turn people away from rather than toward "the other," and thus away from "the Other" as well. There was an article in the *New York Times* a while ago which reported that there are 151 violent conflicts someplace in our world, and that 149 of them are religiously related. Isn't it tragic that this great divine breath of life that God placed within us at our core, as the very soul by which we are alive, would ever do anything but draw people together and home to our God, that it would ever turn us against others who are different from us? What a tragedy! Why would my Catholic faith and my claiming of it ever do anything but turn me toward the neighbor in love and with love, and especially toward the neighbor who is other than I, the neighbor who is different from me?

We must be careful, then, to avoid falling into a narrow sectarianism. We must claim our Catholic identity with great ecumenical sensitivity. Certainly we should do so in ways that ground us in our own particularity, and yet, at the same time, convince us of the universality of God's love for all peoples. To claim religious identity in a way that encourages us to think that "we're the only people whom God loves" is tremendously hazardous. Because if God doesn't really love "the other" then we don't need to either. Perhaps I'm more sensitive to this issue because of my own original Irish culture, where I experienced too much sectarian religion—on both sides—and the dreadful violence that it encourages.

Maybe countering sectarian religion was what Jesus intended when he said: "In my Father's house there are many dwelling places" (John 14:2). We all have a home within God's family and Catholic Christianity happens to be our home. Let's claim it and let's cherish it, but never presume upon the dangerous elitism that we're the only people who have a home within God's family.

Andrew Greeley claims that Catholic identity is primarily rooted in the imagination, and he did significant sociological research to establish his thesis. In other words, while Catholicism is a system of beliefs, of ethic, and of worship, its overall effect on adherents is to shape their imaginations. Catholic Christianity gives us a particular outlook, a perspective that shapes how we approach life, and especially our way of responding to its great questions. It colors our imagination in how we respond to questions like: Who do we think we are? What's it all about? What time do we have? Are we made for each other? In what will we invest? Who is our neighbor? What stories will we tell?—the ultimate questions.

When we bring this beloved tradition of ours to these great questions, our imaginations take flight toward great life-giving responses and possibilities. Catholicism lends us a way to bring our lives to our faith and our faith to our lives. In other words, imagination is what enables our Catholicism—at its best—to become a spirituality. I'm convinced that Catholic Christianity does not *have* a spirituality; rather, it *is* a spirituality. It's a way of making faith come alive, of putting faith to work, of bringing our God-consciousness and the way of Jesus to everyday life, to permeate how we live our Mondays and Tuesdays and Wednesdays. And when it's at its best it does so in ways that greatly favor life for all—across the board.

One of the best books ever written on the topic "What Makes Us Catholic" was written by Langdon Gilkey. It's called *Catholicism Confronts Modernity*. Gilkey, a great Baptist theologian, is perhaps the finest living Protestant theologian in North America today. Langdon Gilkey looked to Catholicism and wrote about the things he loves—that was twenty-five years ago and it was a powerful gift to the Catholic community. He was a neighbor looking in and saying: "Look, I'm delighted with all the renewal going on, but don't lose some of those deep structures that are yours and that enrich the whole body of Christ; the whole body of Christ will be the poorer if we lose them." Gilkey was looking in as a brother.

Who Do We Think We Are?*

How does Catholic tradition invite us to imagine who we are? In other words, what is a Catholic anthropology—its

*Let me mention in passing here that I have a book that responds to such questions in depth. I recommend it: *What Makes Us Catholic: Eight Gifts for Life* (HarperSanFrancisco: 2002). (I don't recommend many of my books; but on this one, I wouldn't "wait for the movie.")

understanding of the human condition? Who does Catholicism invite us to imagine we are?

To begin with, for almost 2,000 years now, Catholicism has clung tenaciously to the amazing claim that we are all made in the image and the likeness of God. I say "tenaciously" because there are some Protestant traditions in the Body of Christ who have said otherwise. For example, the Protestant Reformers, and especially their left wing, claimed that we are inherently corrupt, totally depraved in our human condition. At the great Council of Trent, (1545–1563), the Catholic tradition refused this notion of total depravity. It admitted that, indeed, we are capable of terrible sin and evil, but it also said that this is not what defines us. In fact, we are more graced than sinful, more prone to good than evil. Why? Because the divine image has never been lost to us.

Add to Genesis 1 the second creation myth of Genesis 2. There we read that God breathed God's own life into *the person of the earth (adam)* and it became *nephesh,* alive by the very life of God. Isn't it amazing to imagine that this life coursing through our veins is the very life of God; that we are alive with divine life. And in Christian faith, if we needed further assurance of the inherent goodness of the human condition, we find it in the Incarnation—our conviction that God lived among us as one of ourselves in Jesus of Nazareth. How could God possibly take on our human estate if it were inherently sinful; and how could we doubt our own innate goodness after God "became flesh, and lived among us"? (John 1:14)

Now, let us be honest; the inherent goodness of the human condition is our official "party line" but we have often honored this sentiment more in the breach than the observance. The Jansenists, being overly devout Catholics of the right (and throughout Church history, heresy has most often been to the right), tried to convince the Church that we are inherently sinful. And a lot of their influence rubbed off, certainly on Irish Catholics, but on French, and Polish, and others as well. But, in fairness to the Church, it condemned Jansenism as heresy. It simply knew in its depth structures that the divine image is never lost to us, and that Jesus Christ has ultimately affirmed the goodness and Godness of our condition. Though we are originally sinful, even more so, as Rahner spent his life trying to convince us, we're originally graced.

Made in God's image, and alive by divine life, the human condition has its innate dignity. We don't need to earn our dignity and worth; we have these by copyright, as it were. They are free gifts from a loving God. Likewise, this anthropology demands that we recognize the fundamental equality of all people. Catholics must believe and champion the conviction that no one is any more in the image and likeness of God than anybody else. Our faith demands this. No matter the gender, race, sexual orientation, or creed, every person reflects the divine image, is alive by divine life, and is blessed by the incarnation of God in Jesus.

This way of thinking results in a positive anthropology; it encourages us in the conviction that "grace works through nature"—echoing how Aquinas stated this classic Catholic position. In other words, God takes us into partnership to bring about the reign of God. And so, by God's grace we can make an amazing difference for life; we can take and reshape history toward God's reign. For Catholic faith, God will not bring about God's reign without us. God could, but chooses to work with us, to work through us, to take us into partnership, into covenant, if you will. By God's grace and our own best efforts, we have extraordinary potential for good, and for the common good of all.

Such a Catholic anthropology invites us, as Irenaeus expressed it so long ago, to become fully alive to the glory of God. Isn't it lovely to think that the more authentically human we become, the more we give glory to God. Surely this reminds all parents and teachers of the priestly nature of their vocations. Every time you educate and enhance the life of a child, you are performing a priestly function—giving glory to God. For the glory of God is the human person "fully alive."

What's It All About?

Let's take up another great question of life and reflect briefly on how our Catholic Christian faith might prompt us to imagine a response. What's life all about? If the first question "Who are we?" refers to our anthropology, this question brings us to our cosmology—our outlook on life in the world and how we put together a "world" for ourselves.

Again, we have often honored our Catholic cosmology more in the breach than the observance. Yet, we must recognize that, at its best, Catholicism encourages a tremendously positive outlook on life. Our life is a good gift to be cherished and relished, to be celebrated and defended, from womb to tomb. Our life is gracious, meaningful, and worthwhile. Not because we "make" it so, as in the existentialist notion of "making meaning." Rather the worth and worthwhileness of our lives is a gift, a given by God's grace. This life of ours is not a problem to be solved or a burden to be borne, but a gift to be lived with gratitude.

Such a cosmology is one reason why Catholics may have a little more fun—at least on occasion—than people from other traditions. It's why we've never condemned dancing or singing, celebrating or even drinking alcohol. Of course, all such things can be abused or misused, but they're not inherently evil. The great youth ministry poster with which many of us grew up is a powerful statement of a Catholic outlook on life; "God does not make junk." This is true of all of God's creation, including ourselves. Life is a great gift to be lived well and richly celebrated, enjoyed, and defended. My grandmother, God rest her, had a wonderful way of stating a Catholic cosmology, though she'd never have called it that. She was fond of saying, "Every morning you wake up, throw out your arms, and if you don't feel the side of a coffin, that's a great day." Now, that's a Catholic outlook on life!

The core aspect of Catholic tradition that expresses even as it encourages this attitude toward life is our *principle of sacramentality*. Too often, Catholics think of sacramentality solely as what we do in Church, as when we celebrate the seven sacraments. But the seven sacraments in church are no more than the high point celebrations of the whole sacramentality of life. The sacramental principle is this extraordinary conviction *that God comes looking for us and we respond to God through the ordinary "stuff" of everyday life.* The Catholic sacramental principle enables us to find the divine in the human, the ultimate in the ordinary, the more in the midst of every day. As the poet Gerard Manley Hopkins expressed it, all creation is "charged with the grandeur of God"; to a Catholic imagination, all is sacramental.

This is why we have the audacity to show up in our churches and to believe that our God comes looking for us through bread and wine, through water and oil, through the Word and assembly, and through lovemaking in marriage. Indeed, remember the old Catholic theology of marriage which claims that the sacrament is not effected at the altar but in the honeymoon bed when that couple makes love. The sacramentality resides in the act of lovemaking. (Note the potential here for a much more positive spirituality of sexuality than the one on which most of us were raised.)

Within our whole sacramental economy, Eucharist, of course, is what Aquinas called *sacramentum sacramentorum*—the sacrament of sacraments. Eucharist is this extraordinary encounter between the divine and human. At one level, it is simply bread and wine. But to the Catholic imagination, this is the body and blood presence, the real presence, of the Risen Christ to us. Ah, but Eucharist is not only the summit but also the source of our imagination and faith (Vatican II, *Constitution on the Sacred Liturgy*, 10). As a source, what does Eucharist invite us to imagine about life? To quote Ignatius of Loyola, "To see God in all things." Or with the poet Patrick Kavanagh, "To find God in the bits and pieces of everyday." This is the faith outlook on life, the imagination, to which Catholicism invites us.

Are We Made For Each Other?

In *What Makes Us Catholic* I reflect on eight of the great questions of life; here I raise up just some highlights in response to three of them. Our third fundamental question is, "Are we made for each other?" If the first question above refers to our anthropology, and the second to our cosmology, this one raises up our sociology. So, does Catholic imagination encourage a particular perspective on our *socius*, our relational life? The answer is a resounding "Yes." It assures us that we are indeed made for each other?

When God confronted Cain with the whereabouts of Abel, Cain asked rhetorically, "Am I my brother's keeper?" In many ways, the remainder of the Bible is an overwhelming response to this sociological question. It renders a resounding "Yes"—we are our brothers' and sisters' keeper. This sociology is contrary to an individuality whereby I take care of myself alone—as long as I don't infringe upon the rights of others—a la John Locke. Such individualism is indeed deeply embedded in this great American experiment. But Catholic Christianity calls us to another kind of sociology. It stimulates imagination to see ourselves as essentially relational; ever "persons-in-community" and "a community of persons." And it's not that we're first individuals and then enter into a contractual relationship for mutual benefit. Rather, we are inherently relational; we become who we are through relationships. In God's great divine plan, we indeed are "made for each other."

Personally, I am coming a bit late to parenting, and what an amazing experience it is; with so much potential for insight and wisdom—as well as holiness of life. And as I watch little Ted's personality emerge, I'm realizing in a whole new way that Ted will become the person he becomes primarily out of his relationship with myself and his mother Colleen, and then from his sociality with the other people he will meet along the way. We are essentially relational beings; relationships are not simply incidental but necessary to being human, to being religious, and certainly to being Christian.

Even the word "person" signals that we are made for relationship. It comes from the Greek *prosopon,* which means "to turn toward another." Etymologically, then, "person" signals someone who is always already in relationship. This is in contrast to the word individual—from the Latin meaning to "stand alone." Catholicism asks us to imagine ourselves as "persons"—always and inherently relational—rather than as "individuals." Note well that the Greek word for someone who tries to stand alone is *idiote*—idiot.

Here we have a clue to a deep structure of Catholic Christianity, and to why we put so much emphasis on Church. I have good Protestant friends who would say, "too much so," and they have a point. We Catholics can fall into a kind of "church-idolatry"—forgetting that it's only a means to an end—and make it an end in itself. Surely the dreadful scandal we've been through has some kind of institutional idolatry at its root. But, likewise, perhaps it can now disabuse us of our church inflation. This rude awakening may help us to refocus the church in perspective; to cherish it as a means but not an end. Such nuance notwithstanding, the fact remains that the communal emphasis of Catholicism is not a choice for us; ecclesial identity is essential to being Catholic Christians.

Our emphasis on Church as community flows over into how we understand our way of being in society. In a sense, our ecclesiology shapes our sociology as well. So, we're convinced that we must work together in society for the common good, that each one should contribute according to their means and receive according to their needs. Our ecclesiology is echoed in Catholic social teaching which places so much emphasis on the common good. This claims that there can be no dichotomy between my personal good and the good of all; and both are my responsibility.

Catholic emphasis on the communality of human existence, and of Christian faith, has a powerful instance in its age-old conviction that the bond of baptism is never broken, not even by death. We are deeply convinced, as the Preface of the Mass of the Resurrection states, that for the dead, "life is changed, not ended." We have this deep conviction that we are ever surrounded by a great communion of saints, supporting and praying for us. In Catholic faith, the dead are not nearly as dead as first reported. So, just as I often requested my mother when she was alive, "Ma, say a prayer for me," I could still make the same petition of her this morning. And she can still intercede for me.

Our faith is not that the saints can answer our prayers; only God can do as much. But we can ask them to pray with us, to pray for us, to take our own prayers to God. And because they're in the presence of God, their prayers for us are all the more effective. Of course, this is a very human approach to God, but then God made a very human approach to us, coming among us as one of ourselves in Jesus. Read Elizabeth Johnson's beautiful book on the communion of saints, grounded in this conviction that the baptismal bond is never broken, not even by death.

Fair enough regarding my saintly mother, but then how about my Uncle Tom? One never speaks ill of the dead, of course, but if I've ever known a person who might not have been immediately ready for the beatific vision it would be my Uncle Tom. He died a few years ago and will not be remembered for his piety. Might I leave it at that and say no more? No, I can pray for him. I can perform an act of love, an act of justice, an act of peace, in his name. I can have Mass celebrated for his eternal rest. Somehow—and we should claim no more than that—Uncle Tom will be ready for God and God will be ready for Uncle Tom. Again, I raise up this aspect of Catholic tradition only to make the point that we take communality so seriously that we're convinced it transcends the grave. As the *Catechism* summarizes, "Since all the faithful form one body, the good of each is communicated to the other" (947). And this "works both ways" in the "communion" between us.

Let me close with a reflection on Mary—with a bit of imagination fueled by some Gospel memories of her—because she rightly holds pride of place among the communion of saints. And why wouldn't she? Look at the wonderful son she and Joseph raised. We are surely in need of some balance now regarding Mary. We've been on a bit of a roller coaster with her, from exaggerated devotion, corrected by Vatican II and especially by its liturgical reforms, to nigh total neglect, at least among more liberal Catholics. It's surely time for us to reach a balance and return to this "mother in faith" for who she was and can be in our spirituality.

Wasn't she the first to place Jesus in the tabernacle of the world, in the tabernacle of her own womb, this poor teenage girl, pregnant out of wedlock, who soon thereafter had her child threatened with slaughter and became a refugee to protect him? Yet through it all, and likely with great anxiety about the mystery before her, she remained a woman of faith, saying "Let it be done unto me according to God's word." And look again at the Magnificat for the kind of God she believed in. Mary's was a God who puts down the mighty from their thrones and exalts the lowly, who raises up the lowly, feeds the hungry, and sends the rich away empty-handed.

Where do you think Jesus got his values? Where did he get his extraordinary care for the poor, his outreach to the marginalized, his catholicity that welcomed prostitutes and tax collectors and all kinds of sinners to the table? Where did he get his passion for peace, for justice for the downtrodden? Now you could say, "Well, he was the Son of God." But that would be cheating. Indeed, as the Council of Chalcedon clearly stated, he was fully divine and fully human. But that dogma of our faith also insisted that the two natures never interfered with each other; that the divinity did not compromise his humanity. Jesus wasn't pretending to be a baby in Bethlehem or to be a victim dying a painful death on the cross. Truly, "the Word was made flesh" in Jesus and "dwelt amongst us" (John 1:14). He suffered a terrible death on the cross. So, if the divinity did not compromise the humanity, we realize that he had to be raised and educated like the rest of us.

With this, we recognize anew the extraordinary parents that Mary and Joseph must have been. What a love there must have been between them! How else could he have preached his radical version of the great commandment, a love that reaches even to enemies? Why did he come into the synagogue at Nazareth at the beginning of his public ministry—according to Luke—be invited to read, and choose the text from Isaiah, chapter 61:1–2? "The spirit of the Lord GOD is upon, me, because the LORD has anointed me; he has sent me to bring good news to the oppressed, to bind up the brokenhearted, to proclaim liberty to the captives, and release to the prisoners; to proclaim the year of the LORD's favor." Surely Mary and Joseph had nurtured him in such values.

I love Luke's story of the finding in the temple; surely this is one of the most underreported events in the life of Jesus. Taking this text at face value, it says the boy has been missing for three days. Just imagine their panic and anxiety as Mary and Joseph searched frantically for their only child, in a dangerous city, and they from a remote village in Galilee. Luke says that upon finding him in the temple, Mary simply asked, "Son, why have you done this to us? Your father and I have sought you with anxiety." Now I don't think that's what happened at all. Pardon me, Luke, but I think Mary likely charged into the temple upon sighting her child, scooped him up in her arms and smothered him in hugs and kisses, with "Oh, my God, are you all right? We've been so worried about you? Did anybody do anything to you, anybody harm you? Have you had anything to eat? Oh, my God, we've been worried sick about you."

Then Jesus, it would seem and as twelve-year-olds can do, made some kind of smart-aleck remark like, "Ma, you should've known I'd be in the temple." I'd put my life on it that at that point Mary lost it, and went into a tirade at the kid. Do you think I'm exaggerating? Well, the very next verse in Luke says: "And he went down to Nazareth and was obedient to them." I bet he was. That poor lad was so scared he didn't leave home again until he was thirty. Then the next verse says: "And Jesus increased in wisdom and in years, and in divine and human favor" (Read the whole story in Luke 2:41–52). Well, who raised him and nurtured him in the values that have inspired and challenged the world ever since?

Remember Mary at the wedding feast of Cana. She seems to have been the one most concerned about the possible embarrassment to the young couple. He wondered what business it was of hers or of his. He thought his time "had not yet come." But Mary thought otherwise, and said, "Fill the water pots." As much as to say, "He'll be ready." And he was—real fast. What son or daughter has not known such moments of motherly persuasion, but also a mother who saw in us potential that we didn't even see for ourselves.

I'm totally convinced that Mary was at the Last Supper. Now you don't have to agree with me, of course—I know she wasn't there for the photo. But think about it. Luke 2 says that the Holy Family had a custom of going up to Jerusalem every year for the Feast of Passover. And here she was with him again that Holy Thursday—we know because she was at the foot of the cross the next day—and for Passover, the most sacred and family-centered celebration in the Jewish calendar. Can you imagine a good Jewish son assembling for the Passover meal with his community and telling his mother to wait outside? And can you imagine a good Jewish mother who would tolerate such behavior from her son? Not that this settles any of the current arguments in the Church. But I'd put my life on it: Mary was there.

She was at the foot of the cross next day. Just imagine the dreadful suffering Mary experienced as she witnessed her only son die this terrible death. John's gospel portrays Jesus' concern about his mother's welfare even in the midst of his own terrible pain. As well he might. Most likely, Joseph was dead by now and without a son she would have faced great hardships. So he hands her into the keeping of the "beloved disciple." Maybe this is enough inspiration to take from this text: to care for the poor among us even when we're in pain ourselves. Now, as then, the poorest of the poor are women, and so are their children.

Our Church has long taken this text to represent a symbolic handing over of Mary to the Church as our Mother in Faith. And surely she is. And what more title do we need for her than "Mother in Faith"? And, of course, she was there at Pentecost in the upper room. Acts 2 says that the Spirit descended upon all there present. In other words, Mary and the other women disciples present were as much empowered by the Spirit as anyone else there. Let us ask her to intercede for a Church that recognizes as much for its women today. And let me ask two more questions for reflection and conversation:

- How do these "deep structures" of Catholicism stimulate your own imagination?
- What decisions do they invite for your own faith, for your ministry?

I begin each chapter in my book *What Makes Us Catholic* with a story that's somewhat of a parable representing what the chapter is about. I begin the chapter "What's it all about?" with a story called "A Bit of Good." I include it here because I think it's a good example of what we're all about.

When I rented the car at Dublin airport, they said it was brand new, and sure enough it was. When I headed back to the airport five days later, after two seminars that had gone very well and a delightful visit with my family, the last thing in the world I expected was car trouble. The sun rose slowly on a lovely autumn morning, phasing the Wicklow Mountains into focus on the horizon. Birds were singing among the last of the autumn leaves and I was humming along. About a half an hour from the airport I thought I saw steam rising from under the hood, but I assumed it was the dew vaporizing in the morning sun. Then the temperature gauge rose to boiling point and as I pulled over, the car cut out, enveloped in a cloud of steam. No phone or gas station was in sight. I had to make that flight or I would miss my class next morning at Boston College, my restricted air ticket would be useless. I stood beside the steaming car looking plaintive but I doubted anybody would stop.

Then, to my surprise, an old red Ford Escort pulled over. The driver, a weatherworn middle-aged man by himself asked me in a thick Dublin accent, "Are you in trouble?"

I explained my plight and he said, "Hop in," nodding to the seat beside him. I grabbed my luggage and we were off.

My good Samaritan was Joe Carroll, an old Dub, he said proudly, on his way to work on a building site. I asked Joe to drop me at the nearest village where I could call a cab, but Joe rejoined, "No, there's none out here at this hour of the morning. I'll drop you at the airport."

I protested feebly that it was out of his way.

Joe said, "Yeah, 'tis, but not that much." And then he added "Besides, I've got a daughter in New York," as if that explains something.

Much relieved, I accepted with, "Well, Joe, I'll pay you."

Joe inquired, What county was I from? What brought me back to Ireland? What kind of seminars was I giving? When he heard I was some kind of a theologian, Joe fell silent for a while and then he asked, "So what's it all about?"

I faltered. I said, "whhaaa . . . what's what all about, Joe?"

He said, "Life. The whole damn thing doesn't amount to anything," and he gave a kind of half-circle wave to the horizon.

Since my mentioning theology seemed to prompt Joe's question, I stumbled around about how faith can help us to respond to the graces of life, to find

happiness, to find meaning, to find purpose—
otherwise, it can all seem a bit absurd.

But then, relishing and rising to the occasion, Joe
wanted to know, "What do you mean by faith? What
do you mean by happiness? What do you mean by
meaning?" And then whether all these things had
anything at all to do with going to church.

I was happy to reach the airport. I thanked Joe
profusely. I told him that he was living proof that the
old hospitality hadn't been lost at all. I insisted on
paying him at least what I would have paid a taxi.

Joe refused. He said "Ah, I can't take your
money."

I was adamant.

Whereupon Joe pleaded with me, "Ah, for God's
sake, don't ruin the first bit of good I did today."

With that I had to relent. Joe and I said goodbye
like old friends. As I hurried away to drop off the keys
at the rental company, tell them where to find the
broken-down car, and go to catch my plane, I turned
around and Joe was still there, as if he was seeing me
off. I called back to him. I said, "Hey, Joe, I think you
already know what it's all about."

Joe just gave a soft chuckle and waved again a soft
circle to the horizon.

For Reflection

✧ In your own life, how does being Catholic give you the tools you need for a life close to God?

✧ What customs or traditions does your parish community have which lead people to want to become members? Why would someone become a new member of your parish community?

✧ Beyond the parish, how does your local community benefit from having your parish within it?

Diane Lampitt

Imagining as Fuel for Catechesis

I WOULD LIKE TO DEDICATE THIS CHAPTER TO someone who has been my mentor and teacher. It was in her course, "The Aesthetic Dimension of Religious Education" at Boston College more than fifteen years ago, where I first encountered the power and the role of the imagination in catechesis. To honor her contribution to religious field education, and in gratitude for what she has given to me, I dedicate this reflection to Maria Harris.

What is the Imagination?

Let's begin by taking a look at our sense of imagination and how imagination is fuel for catechesis. *Webster's Dictionary* defines imagination as: "The act or faculty of forming mental images." The *Dictionary of Philosophy* describes imagination a little differently: "Imagination is the process by which we can say that an image is present to us." So imagery and imagination have an essential role to play in all forms of thinking.

Imagination is not simply our capacity to form images; it is our capacity to think and see in a particular way. It involves our capacity to think, it enables us to imagine the possible instead of just the actual.

Cardinal John Newman wrote that faith begins not in a notion or concept but instead in image and symbol. We experience conversion by connecting with, by encountering, the "mystery"—God and Jesus and the Holy Spirit become real to us through this sense of imagination, through this realm, this spark made real within us.

While visiting Germany recently, my husband Scott and I had the opportunity to visit the places where Hildegard of Bingen was educated, served her community, and founded a monastery. It was so interesting to visit the monastery and to walk up the hill to the church where she had prayed and gathered. While we were up on this one particular hill, looking down on the Rhine and this gorgeous scene, and walking around these outdoor Stations of the Cross that are now located there, Scott found this beautiful feather. He picked it up and handed it to me, and I put it in my purse and carried it with me the whole day. For some reason, I didn't want to throw it away.

We walked a little further around the town of Bingen and found this wonderful museum that had a whole section dedicated to Hildegard. We walked in and noticed this gorgeous bronze statue of Hildegard. At the base of the statue, lying by Hildegard's foot, was a rather large feather! And I thought, *That's really strange, what's with the feather?* We walked a little bit further and discovered a special showing of Hildegard's life that was appearing at the local gallery. We saw some pictures and some icons and there, in an icon-like painting of Hildegard, appeared this feather! And I could only think, *What in the world?* So I started asking people about the significance of the feather for Hildegard? Unfortunately, because of the language barrier, people didn't really understand what I was asking, but I kept the feather and I brought it home with me.

When I got home, I got on the Internet and I looked up Hildegard to find out the story behind the feather. Here's what I found. It seems that Hildegard wrote this story about a king. She said:

> Listen, there was once a king sitting on his throne. Around him stood great and wonderfully beautiful columns ornamented with ivory, bearing banners of the king with great honor. Then it pleased the king to raise a small feather from the ground, and he commanded it to fly. The feather flew, not because of anything in itself but because the air bore it along. Thus, I am a feather on the breath of God.

I immediately knew when I read that story that it was no accident that Scott found that feather that day. And it was no accident that I would go and discover what Hildegard had known, which perhaps was God's message to her, because that's the message I hear from God to me, that I am but a feather on the breath of God. It's so freeing to me. I wish I could live it and embrace it at every moment. This is the role of the imagination, this is what imagination does for us. Story, image, symbol, ritual—the meaning is within them. And when we break it open, our life experience connects breaks open and goes deeper. Through imagination Hildegard is speaking to me across the ages and her message is powerful!

In my reading on imagination, I found Andrew Greeley's book, *The Catholic Imagination* (University of California Press, 2001). Father Greeley writes: "Catholics see the holy lurking in all creation. As Catholics, we find our houses and our world haunted by the sense that objects and events, persons and daily life are revelations of grace. This special Catholic imagination can appropriately be called sacramental. It sees created reality as a 'sacrament,' that is, a revelation of the presence of God."

As I think about imagination and the role of imagination and reflect on the world and our world situation, I realize the lack of imagination we have as a country, as a world community, as a church. I realize that it is in the realm of the imagination that we can literally turn swords into plowshares, that we can find a place renewed and filled with hope, leading people to live in the reign of God. For me, imagination is the place where God's revelation and human experience touch.

WITH THE ABOVE REFLECTION on imagination as background, I would like to turn to an exercise on imagination, and in particular on metaphor. It is an exercise in developing a metaphor for catechists. Since in some ways we're all catechists, whether we're working with young people or adults, whether we're working with the Rite of Christian Initiation for Adults or elementary programs, whether we're directors or coordinators, we're all catechists in some way.

This is a very simple, reflective exercise, and it will help you tap into the imagination. Use the formula below and try to come up with a metaphor for catechist—name that metaphor. On the second line, name some of the qualities of whatever metaphor you choose for catechist. For example, let's say that you're working on a metaphor for God. You might say, for example, God is like a tree. What are some of the qualities of a tree? Trees are . . . strong . . . living . . . bendable . . . rooted. To complete the exercise, God is those things too. Take a moment and use this process to come up with your own metaphor for catechist. Then, reflect on the qualities of your metaphor and see if it connects with catechists.

A catechist is something like (a) _____.
_____s are _____/_____/_____/_____.
Catechists are _____/_____/_____.
A catechist is a _____ metaphorically!

Here are some actual sample metaphors. See if you would have ever thought of these. A catechist is like a:

- Rainbow—colorful, multiprismed (multilayered,) solidly transparent, symbols of God's covenant, made up of stardust
- Storyteller—creative, imaginative, brave, funny, smart, verbal
- Fish—varied, can live in different water types, adaptable, lives in schools or communities, and is dead out of water (like a catechist is dead without the living water of faith)
- Bridge—linking heaven and earth
- Carnival barker—calls people in, welcomes them, storyteller, jovial, informative, and holds up expectations

Look at what finding a good metaphor can uncover about being a catechist. After reviewing your own metaphor for catechist, reflect on it through the lens of these questions:

- What are its strengths and limitations for the catechist?
- And what are its strengths and limitations for the learner?
- How has this metaphor opened you up to new ways of seeing your ministry as a catechist?

When you look more deeply at your metaphor you will also find limitations, but it will help you to see the broader, deeper dimension to the role of catechist. This is the purpose of metaphor, to open us to new ways of seeing—just know that there are limits to any language or words that we use. The role of metaphor is extremely important. Think of Scripture as metaphor, as an opportunity for us to go deeper into meaning. The more we play with metaphor, the more comfortable we become with metaphor, the better we are going to be as catechists, with helping our learners open doorways for themselves.

The Use of Story

It was during the course with Maria Harris that I mentioned before, "The Aesthetic Dimension of Religious Education," where I first heard this story from Annie Dillard's book *Pilgrim at Tinker's Creek* (Perennial, 1998). It goes like this:

> When I was six or seven years old, growing up in Pittsburgh, I used to take a precious penny of my own and hide it for someone else to find. It was a curious compulsion; sadly, I've never been seized by it since. For some reason I always "hid" the penny along the same stretch of sidewalk up the street. I would cradle it in the roots of a sycamore, say, or in the hole left by a chipped-off piece of sidewalk. Then I would take a piece of chalk, and, starting at either end of the block, draw huge arrows leading up to the penny from both directions. After I learned to write, I labeled the arrows: SURPRISE AHEAD or MONEY THIS WAY. I was greatly excited, during all this arrow-drawing, at the thought of the first lucky passerby who would receive in this way, regardless of merit, a free gift from the universe. But I never lurked about. I would go

straight home and not give the matter another thought, until, some months later, I would be gripped again by the impulse to hide another penny.

It is still the first week in January, and I've got great plans. I've been thinking about seeing. There are lots of things to see, unwrapped gifts and free surprises. The world is fairly studded and strewn with pennies cast broadside from a generous hand. But— and this is the point—who gets excited by a mere penny? If you follow one arrow, if you crouch motionless on a bank to watch a tremulous ripple thrill on the water and are rewarded by the sight of a muskrat kit paddling from its den, will you count that sight a chip of copper only, and go your rueful way? It is dire poverty indeed when a man is so malnourished and fatigued that he won't stoop to pick up a penny. But if you cultivate a healthy poverty and simplicity, so that finding a penny will literally make your day, then, since the world is in fact planted in pennies, you have with your poverty bought a lifetime of days. It is that simple. What you see is what you get (pp, 15–16).

It's a beautiful, powerful story of imagination, of seeing. About two years after reading that story in class, I found myself in a kind of dark night of the soul—depressed, not knowing where I was going, and feeling really bad about myself. I was seeing a wonderful spiritual director at the time, who was really trying to help me through this pathway of finding myself at a deeper level. I had just finished my appointment with her, left her office, and gone out to my car in the parking lot—and I had been crying. I put my key in the car door and looked down, and what did I see but a penny? I picked up the penny and immediately the story from Annie Dillard came gushing back to me, flowing into my consciousness and my imagination, and I felt this kind of flutter of happiness amidst all of my sadness.

I remember sloughing it off—it was just a penny. I got in my car, put the key in the ignition and started the car, and looked in the rearview mirror. Completely covering the back of my car behind my back seat under the back window were all these pennies—There had to be twenty or thirty pennies; I couldn't believe it—all just thrown in the back of my car. I looked at them and I just remember laughing hysterically, and then I'm crying and them I'm laughing and then I'm crying, and I'm thinking to myself, *God is saying to me, Diane, I love you. Why does it matter?* It was such a powerful experience for me. . . . Of course, I found out later on that a friend of mine said it was good luck when you get in a new car to throw money in it, which is what he had done. But it didn't matter how the pennies got there; that wasn't the point. The point was what it evoked within me at a time when I needed it the most—that sense of story, how story comes back to us, how story embraces us, and how story connects us with the holy in such a profound way.

Here's an exercise to use with story. Take a moment to reflect on a story, maybe the story by Annie Dillard, or maybe a story of an experience of God's revelation in your own life, a story of when you encountered the holy in a very special way. How does this story speak to you? Reflect on how the story opens you up to continued conversion. Here's the process:

- How does this story speak to you?
- What stories do you have of God's revelation in your life?
- How does story open you up for continued growth/conversion?
- How is story fuel for catechesis?

Stories can make us laugh, make us see the other side of the story, and open us up to other perspectives. Stories can make us cry, put us in touch with our real selves, our emotions, our affective life. Stories have the power to surprise us, captivate us, make us think. They help us to relate, to relive events, bring us back to our childhood and take us to all kinds of places. Stories are like windows. Stories give us the sense of us; we are not alone. The telling of stories opens us up to new ways of thinking and in the retelling of stories we continue to grow from the same stories.

The power of stories is not just in the telling of our stories but in the listening to stories and the breaking open of stories, because the more we break open the stories the deeper we find meaning within them. Sometimes stories are wonderful because they catch us by surprise and they shock us into a new way of seeing. Sometimes stories are subtle and it's in the retelling of the story that we continually uncover deeper meaning for ourselves. And sometimes stories are a little too familiar, so we have to look at the stories afresh and anew in order to continually discover what's within them. Story has this powerful capacity for opening us up to continue to conversion, to new ways to recognize the holy in the ordinary.

The Visual Arts

In addition to metaphor and story, look at art and the artistic process, and form. Take, for example, Andrew Rublev's icon of the Holy Trinity. This icon was painted at the height of the icon tradition in Russia during the 1400s. With all icons, every paint-stroke contains meaning hallowed by the people who have gone before; the prayer of the centuries continues through the eyes of that artist. Looking at an icon is like looking through a window out from the obvious realities of everyday life into the realm of the holy, into the realm of God. An icon puts color and shape to that which cannot be grasped by the intellect, rendering visible that which is invisible, which is what a sacrament does. It is sacramental.

The story taking place in this particular icon by Rublev is the mysterious story of Abraham receiving three visitors as he camps under the oak. He entertains the three visitors and serves them a meal. As the meal and the conversation progress, Abraham realizes that he is talking straight to God, and that somehow these "angels" are in some way a metaphor for the three persons of the Trinity. (As an exercise, find this Rublev image of the Holy Trinity on the Internet and reflect on what this icon says to you about the Trinity.) Henri Nouwen wrote this wonderful reflection on Rublev's icon:

> Andrew Rublev painted this icon not only to share the fruits of his own meditation on the mystery of the Holy Trinity but also to offer his fellow monks a way to keep their hearts centered in God while living in the midst of political unrest. The more we look at this holy image with the eyes of faith, the more we come to realize that it is painted not as a lovely decoration for a convent church, nor as a helpful explanation of a difficult doctrine, but as a holy place to enter and stay within. As we place ourselves in front of the icon in prayer, we come to experience a gentle invitation to participate in the intimate conversation that is taking place among the three divine angels and to join them around the table. The movement from the Father toward the Son and the movement of both Son and Spirit toward the Father become a movement in which the one who prays is lifted up and held secure (*Behold the Beauty of the Lord,* Ave Maria, 1987, pp. 20–22).

Nouwen gives us this wonderful expression of what happens in art, in all forms of art, that we are invited into the piece, to be in conversation—this icon especially invites us into intimacy with the Trinity. What's interesting is that icons can be used to express doctrine. Think about what we do in our classes, how we teach about the Trinity. Here, in a piece of art, three angels are sitting around a table, openly inviting one in to conversation, to be a part of the dynamic of the Trinity. The picture evokes all of what we're trying to say the doctrine of the Trinity holds within it. When we use the imagination, when we use artistic forms, we allow the artistic forms to evoke the meaning and then our doctrine affirms that meaning. It's wonderfully expressed in this particular icon.

MY HUSBAND SCOTT started creating metal sculpture nearly ten years ago. He's a landscaper by trade and found himself making repairs on different equipment and trailers and doing some welding. He collected different metal pieces that had been thrown away and he started making new shapes and forms out of the discarded metal. As he started experimenting with this, I was working as a DRE in a parish at the time and I said, "Scott, what would you think about creating a bucket for the fire at the Easter vigil?" I explained how we made this fire and what we needed, and I commissioned him to create a container for the fire at the Easter vigil.

Scott found a fifty-gallon drum and cut out flames and welded them back on in different positions, allowing the flames to be seen from all directions, and he built a stand. At the Easter vigil we put this fire bucket outside the church and lit the fire and it was a glorious fire. It was incredibly powerful and moving for Scott to see the imagery of his prayer and reflection as he created it now being used in this context. But what hit him even more than the fire when we began the liturgy was what he saw when we were leaving the church about two hours later, after the vigil. As we walked out, the embers of the fire were glowing so brightly that the image of those flames that he had cut out were now the image of that fire within us.

Scott was so moved by this experience that he started working more and more with metal forms and he decided that he wanted to create more with metal. Today, he does his metal sculpture pretty much full-time and has his art in several galleries. Creating pieces of art out of discarded metal has become his source of prayer. I want to share with you his philosophy statement because he feels it is an important dimension of his artistic expression:

> These new elements were created out of my conviction and concern for all of God's creation. They have been created out of old elements, thrown away and discarded by others. For the life of the world, they have been created anew. These art pieces were inspired by the Spirit who was present at the dawn of creation and who will continue to work through us as faithful stewards of this earth.

How powerful this is, this sense of not making something new, but of taking something that was already there and through our imaginations creating it anew. This is exactly what Scott does. When he picks this metal up from the junkyard, who sees anything in it? I don't. But somehow as he's creating—and he really believes it is the work of the spirit within him that creates—new and beautiful images emerge. In so many ways, this is our work as catechists, to be facilitators to helping us see what others don't see—not that everything is junk and that we create it anew, but that we have new possibilities and connections and ways of drawing out reality to lead people into the future. Both art and the artistic process lend themselves to helping us to continue to grow in imagination. so consider these questions:

- How does art speak to you?
- How do the arts and the artistic process open us up for continued growth and conversion?
- How is art fuel for catechesis?

Art can invite you into the ministry of God. Art makes you look a little closer, a little deeper, get beyond the surface. Art is more than just an intellectual approach, it is more holistic. Cultivating art is cultivating this way of seeing that all of life contains what is holy. If we only had eyes to see this—and we do—our role as catechists is always uncovering and assisting others to see what is holy. Art evokes feelings. Think of the balance of who we are, not just about the feeling level. Story and metaphor and art tap into a place that isn't as controlled as our minds. We have a way of really filtering and making decisions about what categories things belong in when they come through our heads, and when they enter through our affective senses and touch us in such deep ways, we still take it to our minds to make sense out of it and name it and articulate it. So it's never only emotion.

A professor of mine was once talking about heaven in class. Someone was asking about heaven. This professor gave this wonderful explanation that heaven is like an art gallery. Picture yourself in an art gallery. If you're someone who knows nothing of art, who has no appreciation for art, and you walk through that art gallery, you're going to look at the pictures and the paintings of people, and so what? But let's say you're someone who has an appreciation for art. You're not an artist yourself and maybe you don't understand the technique, but you appreciate it. You walk through that art gallery looking at the same exact pictures, but you're taking in something a little bit different, something a little bit deeper.

Now let's say you yourself are a master artist; you've culti- vated the art, you've tried your skill, you've developed, you've studied, and you've worked. Now you are the one walking through that art gallery, looking at these same fine pictures and works of art; you're looking at them with a whole different appreciation. And the professor said that's something like what heaven is. The reign of God is here and God doesn't take that away from anyone. But it's really our way of seeing, our sight, that makes us recognize that we are in heaven. This way of seeing doesn't just do something for us, the way we see translates into our whole being, into the way we act, the way we treat other people, the way we relate to other people. Our way of seeing is really our entire being and it captivates our souls.

Value the Imagination and the Imaginative Process

Our next step is to take some time and reflect on ways we can integrate these reflections into a catechetical setting, suggest some applications. My first suggestion is about valuing the imagination. Based on our reflections on metaphor and story and art, and based on our experiences, how do you feel tapping into the imagination is fuel for your catechetical setting?

Imagination allows us to integrate profound reality into our souls. For many, it is the fullest way to know God. When we value imagination and the role of imagination in our own lives, it translates to our learners, whether they are children, adolescents, or adults. They themselves will begin to value their imagination and the way they see.

Art, music, and poetry engage our imagination in powerful ways. If we open ourselves to their invitation, they are capable of leading us to places where we're able to "see" beyond our rational understanding. Cultivating the imagination is cultivating a way of seeing—and what we see is what we get!

Use the Imagination Intentionally in All Your Catechetical Activity

There's also an intentional use of imagination, how we use stories, how we use Scripture, how we listen to stories. As catechists, it's wonderful for us to be storytellers. But we also need to be story listeners to the people in our groups. By listening we draw the story out of the person. We help people sometimes hear their story for the first time. That's why listening can be so healing. As someone is telling their story and knowing that someone is valuing what they're saying, they are healed, they're transformed through the listener. So intentionally call upon the imagination as storyteller and as story listener.

As someone who helps to break open stories, and because we share as partners with one another as we share our stories, sometimes it takes another person to point out something in our own story that we haven't noticed before. Sometimes someone else can help us find greater and deeper meaning in our own stories. So we all need to be better at breaking open stories and reflecting on stories with one another.

Thinking about the use of metaphor, about Scripture and how Scripture abounds with metaphor, how do we as catechists allow that metaphor to be broken open by learners, by our students, by the adults and participants in our programs and our sessions? As catechists are we equipped to give definitions and meaning? Are we equipped to tell people what things mean? Or, instead of being like midwives, who are patient enough simply to be present, to help people name the experiences for themselves, to be able to share with them the sense of our living tradition, are we catechists who are there ready with the doctrine, providing the meaning? As catechists we need to intentionally take a look at the way we teach, and the setting, and how we allow people to enter into Scripture. Do we allow people to enter into the story and find their own experience there for themselves?

A wonderful example of this is in ritual and it's so profound, whether you work in RCIA or you do sacrament preparation. One of the things I'm most proud of in the new sacrament program that we have developed at RCL is that we put ritual as the opening experience of each chapter. This is not a catechetical ritual with a lot of things to do and prepare, but one primal symbol and primary ritual action. After we celebrate this ritual, we reflect with young people and with adolescents: What was that experience like? What did that mean to you?

We allow the meaning of the symbol and the meaning of the ritual to come out of the life experience of the person. Then we build on that. And we help them to see that our Catholic tradition and our church has a whole treasury of meaning and understanding behind that for them. But we have to be careful in using the imagination to allow the stories to evoke the meaning, and some of us are a little uncomfortable with that. It's a lot easier to say what the answer is in the teacher manual rather than asking people, What did you experience? What was that like for you?

As you look through the curriculum and the materials you use, including, of course, music and dance, be especially careful and thorough. But realize especially that it's you as the catechist who's using and evoking imagination as the fuel and the energy source for people to be in touch with their intimate relationship with God as that grows and continues to grow on their journey.

HERE'S A FUN LITTLE PIECE for you to be in touch with your imagination. It's called "Ten Steps to Enliven the Imagination." I've adapted it from a variety of sources:

1. Listen to music: Music soothes the soul and opens us up to new dimensions. Many artists create while listening to music.

2. Carry a pen and paper: Jot down your ideas, images, and thoughts for contemplation later.

3. Open up the Scriptures, the *Lives of the Saints,* an encyclopedia, even a dictionary: Take in new insights each day! See what you find that connects to your life experience.

4. Exercise, jog, go for walks: Any change in activity is stimulating!

5. Turn off the television and activate your mind. Engage in conversation and challenge your brain with new intellectual pursuits.

6. Read, read, read: Expand your interests and take the time to explore new things. You will revel in the new inspirations you have and the new connections you make.

7. Journal: Put your inner feelings and your thoughts and dreams down on paper. Whether they are expressed in words or images, it is freeing to see what is going on inside!

8. Take care of yourself: Nurturing an attitude of care cultivates reverence and respect for others and ourselves.

9. Take risks: Be courageous; step out and try something new; experiment with different forms, like the great inventors and artists. Political reform happens because of risk-takers. Transformation and reform of all kinds are made possible through risk-taking. Are we willing to

take that risk in our reformation or our renewal of the church?

10. Pray to the Holy Spirit: The Creator Spirit, the Divine Source of Imagination:

Come, Holy Spirit,
Fill the hearts of those who would be faithful,
Kindle in them the fire of Love.

Send forth your Holy Spirit
And they shall be created
And they shall renew the face of the earth.
Amen.

For Reflection

❖ When you stop to think about it, what is your personal dream for your own family or household? What can you imagine happening that would enrich your daily life?

❖ Imagine a way to provide catechesis in your parish that would delight and attract people to it? What elements would be there? What would you stop doing that is in your present programs?

❖ What is the message your parish sends to the neighborhood or town where it's located? How is that message sent? How could it be clearer or more prophetic?

Anthony J. Gittins

Imagining Discipleship

Introduction

A RECENT BOOK OF MINE CALLED *ENCOUNTERING Jesus: How People Come to Faith and Discover Discipleship* (Liguori, 2002) provides the background, the context, and some of the content for this chapter. The book contains seventeen of the encounters between Jesus and individuals that are found in the New Testament. I go through them in order to try to open them up a little bit, to discover what they are saying and what kind of challenge they offer to the people whom Jesus is actually encountering, not to mention on occasion to Jesus himself. Above all, I try to discover what they may mean for us, and to make the application to our own lives.

The book started as a retreat I gave to a group of retired sisters about ten years ago. They seemed to like it. A few years later, when I was asked to do another retreat with a different group, I asked if they would like to look at encounters between Jesus and a variety of people. They seemed interested, so I went ahead. Like the first group, they appeared quite happy about it, too. To my great surprise, people started writing me letters and saying things like "I have been a religious for fifty-five years and I have never known Jesus." I became profoundly distressed or disturbed by this because I asked myself what they had been doing. I wondered what kind of piety they had—some kind of disembodied or a non-encountering spirituality perhaps. I decided that, since they found the retelling of these stories helpful, I would start to write them up—they had only been in the form of notes, or sketches for talks. So I began to write them up, and they became *Encountering Jesus*.

I need to explain to you how I approach discipleship, and then I will use two of the New Testament stories as illustrations.

Thinking Discipleship

My first questions are these: Do we have a satisfactory grasp of what we're called to be and who we're called to be as Christians and disciples? Do we have a *particular* grasp? Not just a general kind of grasp, but do we have a sense of urgency in our own lives, a sense that God is asking us to respond in a certain kind of way? It's been said many times for many years that nobody else can do what you are being asked to do, and if you don't do it then it won't get done. But many of us don't take ourselves seriously and we don't take God seriously, and the consequence is that we tend to think, "I can't do very much at all." That kind of attitude is only just this side of sinfulness!

We are called and made in the image of God to do great things by allowing God to work through us. So *do* we have a satisfactory grasp of God's place in our life and our place in God's, or do we perhaps need to work on it a little? Or perhaps this is *not* where we are at this time. Maybe we are actually too easily satisfied with our life. Maybe we are growing into a certain kind of complacency. Do we actually *not* want to be challenged? Do we *not* want to be turned round? Do we resist our own conversion or even think that we've already been converted? If conversion in our life is only a thing of the past or not something we've ever encountered, then we're not Christians yet. Conversion is something that we need to engage. For a lot of people, even the idea that they would like to engage their own conversion only leads them into a kind of wistful or wishful thinking, because they don't necessarily know how they might direct themselves, or where they would go for a sense of direction.

Meanwhile, right under our noses—almost literally—the New Testament is absolutely filled with extraordinary stories of encounters between Jesus and a huge variety of people. These are life-changing encounters. People are searching for meaning or striving to have some of the pain or void in their life healed or filled up. They discover in their encounters with Jesus not only that their initial problem is addressed and even solved, but that that their current situation provides a springboard to the discovery of an entirely new dimension in their lives.

Henri Nouwen famously talked about being wounded healers. My sense is that this is too modest: We need to become *healed* healers. We need to come and be healed, so that we can then go as healers, because coming to Jesus to be healed is only one part of a cycle. The reason we come to Jesus is *not* only to be healed, but so that we can be sent to heal, all of us. As Tom Groome reminded us, this is our mission by baptism: to be a source or occasion for other people's healing. Actually, it's not our mission, it's God's mission. More properly, we are "co-missioned," called and sent by Jesus as his emissaries, to do Jesus' work and not our own. We are co-missioned by Jesus to continue on earth the mission that he brought down to earth in the first place.

Imagining Discipleship

Before I actually look at a couple of examples I would like to work through an approach to discipleship, an approach that makes explicit use of our imagination. In other words, I am saying that we must become disciples and we can become disciples if we use our tradition, which is the Gospel, and if we use our imagination too. Many people seem to read the Gospel, if at all, with a complete lack of imagination. We need to use our imagination not only in order to find out what is going on in these encounters, but to discover *what on earth it means:* that is, what it means for us, now, on earth.

The purpose of having the treasure that is the Gospel is so that it can speak to our lives today. The Gospel is not an antiquarian book. It is not intended to be observed like the Book of Kells or simply paraded like the Book of the Gospels at Sunday liturgy. Its purpose is to speak a living word to us, to enliven our lives, to be a way to the Way of Jesus, to Jesus the Way, the Truth, and the Life. We can only hear a living word if we are open to it—not just our ears, but our imagination.

I have three themes: first, imagination itself; second, discipleship; and third, coming to faith. This third one in particular will get us intimately drawn in to the business of discipleship so that we're not just looking at other people as disciples, but we're looking at other stories in order to find our way to faith, in order to find out how other people come to faith *so that we may learn wisdom and come to faith ourselves.*

Imagination

The first theme, imagination, is that creative ability to form images using past experience and using our own capacity to visualize. We have to talk about the *active imagination,* an intentional looking at and thinking about and creating from whatever our starting point is. This could be a blank wall, or the face of a friend, or the Gospel itself. We have to engage it in an active kind of way. The creativity of imagination, however, is very largely a gift. I don't know how much you can actually work toward creativity or grit your teeth and become creative. Some people seem to have creativity in their genes and some people don't. All is not lost, however, because this is only part of imagination, but this part is gift. One thing we *can* do, of course, is beg; we can ask for gifts: "Oh God, give me a little bit of imagination." And maybe God will give us a little bit of imagination. If we don't ask, maybe we will continue to not have any.

The second thing about imagination is that it is not just a gift but also a skill. And skills *can be* acquired. So there's a component of imagination that we can acquire. The skill is in recombining things from our previous experience, taking things that don't seem to be related to one another and bringing them together. For example, take a story in the New Testament and take my life right now, and see how the actual story of Jesus' encounter with this person can throw light on my present circumstances and perhaps challenge me as it challenges the person who encountered Jesus. What is being said to this person? How is this person responding? What is the response of Jesus? How is he then modifying the person's response? Where does it all lead? In other words, I can take the reality of my life right now, perhaps with its roots way back in my childhood, and bring this reality to prayer.

How do I pray (already) in this particular circumstance? Or perhaps I've given up on prayer. Let's say I'm suffering at the moment from some level of blindness or deafness or paralysis or bent-over-ness; maybe I can go back into a story that somewhat reflects my own, and reflect on someone else who experienced something similar. Maybe I can see how Jesus comes to that person and changes his or her life. Or I could do it differently. I might just follow the readings of the day, or even take any encounter more or less randomly, and then reflect on how and where it converges with my own life. To do one or other of those things demands a skill. It requires me to recombine pieces of my life imaginatively, as I reinterpret or reapply a Gospel story to my life. It's like a jigsaw puzzling skill, and I can learn it. Skills can be improved and sharpened by practice. But if we don't practice, we don't build up our skills.

The third component of imagination is wisdom. Wisdom is a rare synthesis between knowledge and experience. People with a lot of knowledge don't necessarily have wisdom, and people with a lot of experience don't necessarily have wisdom either. Sometimes you hear people say, "Oh, I know that; I have thirty years' experience." But you can still be unwise, even with a lot of experience! Wisdom is the synthesis between experience and knowledge, so that you merge them and you make of them something that demonstrates not just how much you know but that you have pondered and been modified by knowledge and experience and mellowed by it. Wisdom essentially is not a gift that you hold; it's more like something that is available for other people. You don't show it off. You distill it, if you like, and offer it freely. Sometimes you are completely unselfconscious about it, and that may be the sign of profound wisdom.

So wisdom is a facet of imagination that takes the knowledge and the experience that accrues or is gathered over a lifetime, and slowly begins to reflect upon it and to say, "I'm not as stupid as I think I am; I'm not as dumb as I think I am; (but neither am I as brilliant as I may be tempted to think I am)." The point is that neither experience nor knowledge is enough alone to produce wisdom. You can know all about the Bible and you can know all about theology and this doesn't give you wisdom or faith.

Faces of Discipleship

The second component is discipleship. In the New Testament we have a wide variety of blueprints for discipleship. Discipleship has different faces: Disciples are not clones because discipleship depends on circumstance, context, status, economic means, state of health, or where you are in your life. Discipleship is also a process of conversion. We can identify three components that make it easier for us to ask some questions about discipleship and about ourselves. The three components are encounter, displacement or disturbance, and commission.

Encounter

As Viktor Frankl said a long time ago, "To love you must encounter." You can't love in the abstract because there are no people in the abstract. There's no such thing as generic love because there are no generic people. You can only love by encountering a particular person. You can't love "the poor" because "the poor" don't exist except as a classification or a category. But you can love this poor man or that poor woman. You can't love "the sick," only sick people. You can't love tax collectors and sinners, and Jesus didn't love tax collectors and sinners: Jesus loved this particular tax collector and that particular sinner—one by one, and individually. Jesus' entire life was not directed to loving categories; his entire life was dedicated to encountering people! One of the wonderful ironies in some of these encounters is that you're left asking yourself how much did Jesus encounter that person, how much did that person encounter Jesus, and how much was Jesus himself changed by the encounter, because encounters change both parties. And if they don't change both parties, they're not true encounters.

So we *must* encounter if we are to discover discipleship. We must encounter the master; we must encounter Jesus. We must know Jesus; not just know *about* Jesus. We must know Jesus as we know a partner or an intimate friend. And the way we come to know Jesus requires our imagination, that synthesis between experience and knowledge that produces wisdom. But Jesus calls people to and through encounters that modify the way they behave from then on.

It's become a little trite to ask "What Would Jesus Do?"(WWJD). But beneath the triteness is search for truth. The answer to the question is not something that simply pops into my head and allows me to justify what I was going to do anyway! The question has to arise from my actual encounters with Jesus, in such a way that when I ask it, I'm already committed to changing my behavior. And this, of course, is one of the reasons I don't ask the question as often as I might! If I'm willing to ask the question seriously, then the assumption is that I have a working relationship with Jesus and that Jesus is calling me to do something. (We'll look at a story about this, and see how it may take more than a few minutes to establish such a relationship.)

Another component of encounter requires knowledge of what H. Richard Niebuhr called the "inner history." It's a helpful little phrase, and contrasts with the "outer history." Let's say that you're planning to go to Japan for vacation; you've never been there and you don't know any Japanese or any Japanese people. Well, you may go to the library and you may go online and learn *about* Japan; that's the outer story, or history. And you can learn it quite well, *without any reference to or encounter with Japanese people.*

Some people seem to think that *knowing about* God, or Jesus, is the essence of faith. They've read, and maybe even studied, the Scriptures. They've learned about all kinds of religious things. But what Niebuhr is alerting us to is the fact that we must know the inner history: it's not enough to *know about.* We must actually encounter. And this applies to God, to Christ. When we know this *inner history* or inner story, it's not that we absorb another person or know exactly what it feels like to be them, but that we encounter them and their experience. We can never say, "I know exactly what you mean; I know exactly how you feel." Of course, we don't know *exactly* how somebody else feels when they're pouring out their heart to us. It can be very offensive if we cut in and say, "I know how you feel because it happened to me." Well, it didn't happen to you, and you've never had another person's experience!

Jesus never does this kind of thing. When somebody comes to Jesus or when he encounters somebody, Jesus learns that person's inner history. Then Jesus says outrageous things like, "What do you want me to do for you?" This indicates a profound encounter that results in a willingness to modify his own agenda. It also reminds us why we don't very often ask other people what they want us to do for them. Sometimes we tell them what we're going to do, of course. Sometimes, in our self-importance, *we tell them* what we'll do for them—and we expect them to be grateful! But this is not an encounter; it's more of an imposition, however well-meaning.

That's the inner history. Just a little reminder that in our encounters we should be committed not just to knowing things, and not just to knowing about people or circumstances, but to empathy. This is the possibility of somehow feeling analogously the feelings of the other: feelings of loss, of grief, of worthlessness, of guilt, of shame, of sinfulness. We may not have these feelings initially, but in our encounters we can be so affected and touched by the expression of other people's feelings that we become pressed or squeezed like the grape or the olive, squeezed out with compassion—and this is ministry.

Displacement

The second of the components is displacement or disturbance—and I use this word deliberately. In any true encounter, both people are displaced, sometimes subtly, sometimes more radically. So when we encounter Jesus, we should be displaced or disturbed; this a life-changing encounter. It may very well be that Jesus wants, as it were, to embrace us—to console or encourage us—and tell us that we're doing a really fine job. But at the same time he will always tell us to go, to continue, to persevere and do better: Go and do more, go and do differently, go and do something else, go and attend to this or that.

The displacement or disturbance is a critically important component in the relationships between Jesus and people who encounter him. It's probably worth reflecting that we live in a society that likes to be in as close to total control of everything as it is humanly possible to be. We balk at the idea of transitions. We hate the idea of being disturbed or being *displaced;* we want to be *placed,* in place and not out of place. We want to make our place, to have our place—and, if necessary, we'll build higher walls and put barbed wire on top of them to make sure that we are in our place and that nobody displaces us. But this is incompatible with discipleship. Discipleship requires a willingness to be displaced for the sake of the reign of God. I am not the center of my universe and, unless I am displaced, I will not be available for others; I will not be able to encounter others; I will not be able to be a disciple; and I will not be able to practice my faith. All I will be able to do is to practice my ingrown piety.

The title of another recent book of mine is *A Presence That Disturbs: A Call to Radical Discipleship* (Liguori, 2002), which is why I talk about disturbance as much as displacement. The title itself comes from a very famous poem of Wordsworth that many of you already know. The poem is usually referred to as "Tintern Abbey" and sometimes as "Lines Composed a Few Miles Above Tintern Abbey." The photograph on the book's cover is of Tintern Abbey. I went down there (on the border of England and Wales) several years ago to look at it and to ask myself why Wordsworth wrote these lines. What did Wordsworth feel? Wordsworth was a romantic and a theist probably, but not a Christian in any active way. He had a sense of God's movements in the universe, but not a very articulated personal piety, and yet he could say this:

> . . . I have felt
> A presence that disturbs me with the joy
> Of elevated thoughts; a sense sublime
> Of something far more deeply interfused, . . .
> A motion and a spirit, that impels
> All thinking things, all objects of all thought,
> And rolls through all things. . . ."

Wordsworth is saying that as he pondered and prepared to be overcome by the creative muse of poetry, struggling, if you like, for images, struggling for ideas, he "felt a presence that disturbs" him. Then he goes on and writes this monumental poem, one of the finest poems in the English language.

So I went down to Tintern Abbey in the early morning with the heavy clouds brooding over the broken walls and a watery sun struggling to climb over the hills in the background. And after about twenty minutes of sitting silently, I too felt a presence that disturbed me, in the sense that I knew very surely that I was in the presence of God in the decaying ruins of a monastery built nine hundred years before and destroyed five centuries ago. Yet there was a sense of God's presence living there still.

I felt a presence, a disturbing presence, and it came to me then, that that's exactly what Christian life is all about, that's really what discipleship is. God is trying ever so gently to disturb me, so that God can use me to disturb where disturbance is needed, and what very often happens is either that I want to stop God disturbing me or I want to set the agenda of who and what and under what circumstances I will disturb anyone else. But there has to be a sense of flow, a sense that I have *first* been disturbed by God and by God's love and by compassion, which is *then* the reason for my making a disturbance.

I'm not just talking about the negative side of disturbance; I mean the positive side too. We can disturb people by telling them that they're good! We can disturb them by telling them that they do a wonderful job! This disturbs people, and the first thing they say, especially if they're English, is, "Oh, don't mention it," or, "It's nothing." Some of us have a knee-jerk reaction that prevents us from receiving compliments—we can't cope with them. So this sense of disturbance is also something, I think, that you will identify as you look at the encounters between Jesus and various people.

I believe that if we really want to be disciples we need to pray that God will disturb us. But if we don't want to be disciples, then we should pray that God won't disturb us! Of course, if we were to do that, we'd be praying against God, which is sacrilege or blasphemy—so let's not do that! Instead, let's pray that God will disturb us, and that, in doing so, God will give us the capacity to handle it.

Commission

The final component of discipleship is the notion of commission. As I said, we are called not just to be disturbed but to be commissioned, to be invested with the mission of Jesus. We are to be the ambassadors of Jesus and to go through our lives very, very conscious of this, that we must be very careful not to pursue our own agenda but be instruments of God's agenda. This requires prayer, and it takes us back to the very beginning, to the notion of contemplation and encountering Jesus in the first place.

What I have to say about commission is short but quite important. First of all, we are *called*. A call is radically different from an initiative. We live in a culture—a cult, even—of initiatives. An initiative starts with me. When I take an initiative, by definition *I* determine what *I'm* going to do. But a call comes from someplace else. I may not be entirely sure where it's coming from, so maybe I have to listen again, and it will appear to come from someplace else and from someone else. But a call comes from beyond me, from outside of me, not from inside, or at least it doesn't originate with me. My response to a call implies that I'm not following my own agenda, and that I'm willing to follow the agenda of the one who called. Again, this is going to displace my life radically.

There are many genuinely committed Christians, but some of them use their imaginations, it seems to me, in a way that tries to create and to generate as many initiatives as they can, so there's no time for God to call them—or, at least, no time for them to notice. There's no silence, there's no still small voice, there's just white noise, and God cannot get through the noise. Therefore we cannot respond. We live in the most amazingly noisy world!

We have to find the stillness and we have to ask for the call. The pages of the Bible contain all of those wonderful stories of so many calls, such a range of calls—from Abraham to Mary, to Peter, to Bartimaeus, to the Samaritan woman at the well. Some of them come in the middle of the night, and some come to the wrong people at the wrong time. There are calls that people don't want to attend to, calls that people try to hide from, yet calls that are constantly reiterated until people are seduced by God, and lives are changed and prophets arise in the midst of their people. And, God knows, we need it to happen again, now, in our own lives!

The difference between a call and an initiative is radical, and the purpose of the call is not just to bring me closer to Jesus but *to send me into mission*. Now, let's put this whole thing together and look at how it operates in the New Testament.

Encountering Jesus

When we look at encounters between Jesus and people in the New Testament, we can do a number of things. This is where the imagination comes in. The first is simply to identify the context. What's happening here? Who's involved? Where is it happening? Where is Jesus? Where is he coming from? Where is he going? And what difference does it make to the encounter?

Try to get a sense of location because location is quite important. One of the great images or metaphors of the New Testament is the theme of "the way" or "the road," or being "on the way" or being "on the road." Jesus is on his way to something, to somewhere; discipleship is essentially Jesus calling other people to follow him on his way. Sometimes it's very instructive for us to start off by locating an encounter between Jesus and somebody else in relation to where Jesus actually is. Is he sitting down by the well with the woman, on his way between a hostile place and home? Is he on his way home; is he on his way out of town—where is he? And what happens then in terms of the dynamics of the encounter, given that "the way" is code for the call to discipleship? Those early Christians would be known as followers of *The Way*. So, are we going our own way or going the Way of Jesus? Are you "on the way" or "out of the way" or "off track"?

The second thing to look for is faith. What happens almost always—but with one or two extraordinarily important exceptions—is that the person who encounters Jesus comes to faith through stages: two or three, sometimes four. There is usually a tentative movement toward Jesus, and you can see it in terms of how the individual identifies Jesus. It could be, for example, that the first identification is somewhat similar to somebody saying to Jesus, "Hey, you!" That's not intimate and not very close; in fact, it's rather rude. The question then is how far is it, how long does it take, to get from "Hey, you!" to "My Lord and my God"? There's the movement of faith.

Very often in these stories you can see it quite clearly. The first statement may be a "Hey, you!" The second may be a "Hey, you, Jesus!" or "Hey, you, Son of David!" Then it comes to something else. There are stories that have no stages, because the person already has faith! Some of the most profound encounters don't even have words because the person doesn't say anything at all. But there's certainly a presence there. In other words, they are, almost literally, "all ears." They are there—totally, completely *there*.

All over the world, people of different cultures have tried to define what it means to be human. We ourselves talk about walking on two legs and having language—and sometimes we add things like crying. The ancient Israelites defined being human very simply: being human was having ears. Notice how much Jesus focuses on that. He goes around looking for people with ears. He says, "Do you have ears? Can you hear me? Are you listening?" He's saying, "You look as though you have ears, so why don't you listen? Blessed are those who have ears and hear." Jesus is appealing to the humanness of people and, therefore, some of the more tender moments in Jesus' life are when he opens the ears of the deaf because, when he does this kind of thing, it would be very significant and poignant for his audience. They would know exactly what he is doing: he would be making somebody who was regarded as less than human into a human being!

The same was true of other people, for example, "leaky" people. "Leaky" people were a problem for ancient Israelites because for people operating out of a "purity code" you had to be intact, complete, pure. So if anyone was leaking in any way at all (I have to be theologically correct here) then it would have been very hard for them to feel that God really had much time for them. This would have been particularly true of women, for instance, but by extension it applied to people with diseases, including diseases grouped under the name "leprosy"—which involved secretions.

Jesus seems to have had a penchant for "leaky people" or for anyone who was not quite right. He was living within a purity code and a theological system that said, "Don't you dare reach out and touch, because if you do you'll be contaminated." It's as if his own sense of humor almost allowed him to turn that completely on its head and say, "How can I be contaminated by touching somebody else?" So he turns the idea on its head and goes around "contaminating" them with his own holiness! He spends his whole life touching the wrong people, eating with the wrong people, walking with the wrong people, being with the wrong people, in order to "contaminate" the world with holiness and godliness. But because this is done in the context a stringent purity code, it's not surprising that they scratch their heads and say, "We must do something about this dangerous fellow." Nor is it surprising that they cannot tolerate Jesus because he undermines the whole theological edifice.

But worse: Jesus will not stop there. He will tell people that the theology they have been taught is bad, that they have been given the impression that all this is God's will. But it's not God's will at all! So he will say quite brazenly, "Stand up, be whole, speak, hear, go your way, you are healed." And, all the time, he's telling people that they don't know God yet, that he's come to try to help them encounter God. The God he speaks of is *not* the God their theologians have been constructing.

We need to be aware of some of this when we look at how the people come to their encounters with Jesus and how they move, through stages, to faith in him. Then maybe we can understand why Jesus comes to bring faith or to discover faith, and why he is sometimes amazed not only by the lack of faith, but by the faith he finds. Jesus is not the only one who brings people to faith: sometimes he discovers that God has been there first, and Jesus is encountering people who already have faith.

Let's go to a couple of stories, two stories in the same chapter of Mark's gospel, crafted by a master storyteller. They are placed at opposite ends of the chapter, in kind of apposition. You can look at one, then at the other, and notice some interesting points of comparison. In chapter 10, we have the story of the rich man (sometimes called the rich young man, but there is no indication that he was young, and the text does not say that he was young; it says he was a rich man or a leader). We tend to attribute youth to him, perhaps because we want him to have had a second chance later in life. People say, "You never know; maybe he came back later and changed his mind." The younger we can make him, the better chance he has of getting things right later. So we have this wonderful story of the rich man—and what comes next in Mark's gospel is the story of Bartimaeus.

What we have to do is to look at these stories individually, but also make some comparisons. What do we find here? How does Jesus encounter them? How do they respond? What can I learn and apply to my own life? What does it mean for me *now*? This is where imagination comes in, because if I can activate my imagination with the help of the biblical narrative, then I have something solid that will affect my life anytime I try to do this sort of thing. Mark is a master of compressed narrative, so the stories are almost always short and every single word means something significant. Here is the rich man.

A Poor Rich Man

As he was setting out on a journey, a man ran up and knelt before him, and asked him, "Good Teacher, what must I do to inherit eternal life?" Jesus said to him, "Why do you call me good? No one is good but God alone. You know the commandments: 'You shall not murder; You shall not commit adultery; You shall not steal; You shall not bear false witness; You shall not defraud; Honor your father and mother.'" He said to him, "Teacher, I have kept all these since my youth." Jesus, looking at him, loved him and said, "You lack one thing; go, sell what you own, and give the money to the poor, and you will have treasure in heaven; then come, follow me." When he heard this, he was shocked and went away grieving, for he had many possessions (Mark 10:17–22).

So here we have a story, a poignant story, a sad story, a story that we can read and move on from. But it's a story that we really ought to tarry over, that we really ought to take a moment to interpret for ourselves. It begins as Jesus is setting out on his journey. He's had a night's rest and he's now back on the road. He's looking for people to come on the road with him: he's looking for people who might be committed to going *his* way, to following him along the road *he* is taking, to change their minds about the way their lives are directed.

Suddenly a stranger throws himself at Jesus. This looks very much like an *initiative* on his part. He throws himself at Jesus and he starts the conversation. He seems to have been thinking seriously and is not being merely impulsive—he has a question. He's looking for clarity because he asks a very pointed question. But he also needs to be in control, as we will see. He comes up to Jesus; he has not yet been called by Jesus, and this is what makes this encounter different. Normally, the call precedes the sending; "Come" precedes "Go." This man has come to Jesus, but Jesus hasn't called him to come, so there's a little bit of a problem here. Jesus can't actually say much because this man probably has him around the ankles, and if you throw yourself at somebody and grab them around the ankles they're preoccupied with keeping on their feet! I say this because I have a friend in a mental institution where I was celebrating liturgy one day and, just as I got to the "Lord, I am not worthy," he came out of his bench horizontally and grabbed me around the ankles and screamed in a loud voice, "Lord, I am not worthy!" I said "Tom, go back to your place. None of us is worthy. That's why we're here." It reminds me of this young man coming to Jesus.

Jesus is caught off balance as the man addresses him. He identifies Jesus not by name but as "Good Teacher." That's the first identification: it's rather formal, like "Sir!" and it's followed immediately by a question: "What must I do to inherit eternal life?" The implications of this question are very,

very deep. First of all, he asks, "What must *I* do?" (here's an initiative); and second, "*What* must *I* do?" In other words, "I want an answer. Tell me. Put it in a box. Give it to me as a solution. Give it to me like a catechism that I can remember and control. Give it to me clear and simple."

The trouble is, it's a closed question. Closed questions are those that seek a particular, specific, answer: They are looking for the last word on the subject. But *Jesus never answers closed questions* because the life he is calling people to, and the *Way* he is taking, is not clear and neat and predictable. Anything but! Life and redemption are very open-ended. Things are never absolutely clear and responsibilities are never over. We are called to do whatever we can and not to give up, ever. Jesus will tell people to go, to love their neighbor. But, as for who exactly, precisely, clearly, and unambiguously the "neighbor" is, there is simply no final answer. Jesus will tell people to go and find out, go and look, go and encounter, go and discover that there is no way to decide who is *not* my neighbor. Because in Jesus' world, the rules have changed— *everyone* is included.

This man starts out on the wrong foot, asking a closed question. Jesus begins to respond and to respect where the man is coming from, although it's really not where Jesus wants to take him. Jesus says to him first of all, "You call me good. Why do you call me good?" But this is really a rhetorical question—there's no real answer to it. Only God is good, it is true; but conventionally we call people good. So Jesus' question really doesn't take the man very far. Then Jesus picks up on the question the man asks: "What must I do?" and Jesus forces the questioner to reflect on what he already does and how that relates, or might relate, to discipleship. Jesus says, "You know the commandments;" and the man rattles them off. But it's very interesting to note exactly what he rattles off. He lists all the commandments that have to do with other people, or things, and none that have to do with God! He says that he is aware of what he should do for his neighbor, he knows his obligations in regard to thieving and lying and all the rest. But his relationship with God is not articulated. There's a gap in this man's life. He's a doer, an observer of the law, but not a person in relationship with his God, with his creator. This is his problem, although he doesn't realize it.

He finishes listing all those things. Then he speaks to Jesus again and addresses him again. But it's almost as if he's taken a step backward because this time, instead of saying "Good Teacher," he simply says "Teacher." Does he feel a little insulted to be put through his catechism or to be asked questions like this? After all, he's a sophisticated person. Who is this Jesus, checking him out, testing him? So now it's just "Teacher." It's a little bit more distant, a little less warm. There is no movement toward, but rather a movement away from Jesus. And he is quick to justify himself: "I've observed all of these from my youth." So Jesus' response is quite extraordinary: "Jesus looked at him and loved him." Jesus loved him! He's a good man; his heart is in the right place. He is serious and trying to motivate himself. He is setting his goals. He's doing all of these things that you can do by calculation, the kinds of things you can list with a pencil and a paper. But Jesus, of course, wants to get him away from the pencil-and-paper mentality. Nevertheless, Jesus loves him, and this is the starting point.

As a response, out of love, Jesus says, "You lack one thing." If he could say the same of you and me we'd be on cloud nine. One thing? Just one? That's all? I'm okay for every thing except one? Jesus must have transfixed this young man, telling him he lacked only one thing. And if somebody said that to you, you'd really want to know what the one thing is. But Jesus won't tell him!

The very next word out of Jesus' mouth is the imperative, the command: "Go!" It's very dramatic, very clever of Mark the storyteller, and totally unexpected. He says, "You lack one thing: Go!" and then in the very next breath, "Come." So here is a reversal. Instead of "Come" and then "Go," it's reversed: "Go and then come –and then you will know what the one thing is. Then you will have some idea. So go and find out!"

Then Jesus spells it out. "This is the one thing you have to do: Sell what you have. That's it: Just sell what you have . . . and give to the poor and you will have treasure in heaven! . . . and then come follow me." That's the *one* thing? It's quite a program! But in fact it *is* all of a piece. It's distilled. And it's the answer to the man's question.

The man has tried to get his answer in a way that he could handle it. He was looking for something nice and compact. And Jesus has compressed it so tightly into "Go" and "Come" and "Follow me." It is so, so concentrated that the young man just cannot deal with it. He doesn't have the imagination. He didn't want to follow someone else; he wanted to be in control, to do his thing—with God's approval. He doesn't want to be on the way of Jesus, to follow Jesus on *The Way*. He wants to be justified in the thought that his way is the right way. But Jesus wants to invite him to be a companion, *(com-panĕro)* a sharer of bread, a person who sits at the same table as Jesus. Jesus says, "Come and follow me." And the man's face falls, and he goes away sorrowful because he is a man of many possessions.

There's a really curious irony in this last sentence. He goes away sorrowful because he's a man of many possessions. Most people aspire to many possessions because they're sorrowful. Most people hope that when they get many possessions they won't be sorrowful. But this man goes away sad because *he has many possessions*. The word *miser* in English is just the Latin word for "an unhappy man." A miser is an unhappy man because a miser is someone who has many possessions but no friends, too many possessions but no relationships, no debt, no encounter. Jesus is calling this man to enrich himself by encounter, to enrich himself by relationships, even by debt.

There is a phrase that is used sometimes in biblical terms and sometimes in anthropological terms, and it touches the core of the Gospel: the phrase is "mutual indebtedness." It's antithetical to our way of thinking very often. We don't want to be indebted to anybody! We want to be perceived as someone who gives to people, yes, but we're not as good at receiving from people. We're not as good at holding on to mutuality and mutual indebtedness, knowing that I *do* need you, that you *do* need me, and that's a good thing. We're not too good at that because we want to be clean and clear and clinical—no debt, no dependence. Mutual indebtedness is a description of the Christian community. If we are not mutually indebted, we will become misers, we will become unhappy people. The man in this gospel story is a perfect example of a good, good man who went away sad.

So Jesus goes on *his* way, and the sad, rich man goes on his. Just a few verses later, Saint Mark brings us to another story that may seem quite unrelated:

A Rich Poor Man

They came to Jericho. As he and his disciples and a large crowd were leaving Jericho, Bartimaeus, son of Timaeus, a blind beggar, was sitting by the roadside. When he heard that it was Jesus of Nazareth, he began to shout out and say, "Jesus, son of David, have mercy on me!" Many sternly ordered him to be quiet, but he cried out even more loudly, "Son of David, have mercy on me!" Jesus stood still and said, "Call him here." And they called the blind man, saying to him, "Take heart; get up, he is calling you." So throwing off his cloak, he sprang up and came to Jesus. Then Jesus said to him, "What do you want me to do for you?" the blind man said to him, "My teacher, let me see again." Jesus said to him, "Go; your faith has made you well." Immediately he regained his sight and followed him on the way (Mark 10:46–52).

There it is: the way, the way, the way, and the way! Who's on the way? Who's by the wayside? Who's coming my way? It's very beautifully crafted, and true discipleship is encapsulated in this story about *The Way*. As we begin to open it up, we see a wonderful contrast—or a corrective—to the previous story. We see what was wrong with the "good" rich man and what is right with the "bad" poor man, and then we bring them together and realize that now we understand: We know we've been a "good" rich man or woman, or perhaps a "bad" poor man or woman. So what have these stories to offer us? With a little imagination and a whole lot of faith, we can move forward into discipleship and change the world!

"They came to Jericho." They're *on the way*. Mark then immediately switches to, "As they were leaving Jericho." Jesus is now pursuing his agenda. He has something in mind, something to do. He's going someplace. In other words, if somebody (like Bartimaeus) stops him, he will be interfering with Jesus' agenda. Jesus is leaving. He's a man with a mission. What's going to happen is not only that Bartimaeus will interfere with Jesus' agenda, but that Jesus will actually change his agenda because of Bartimaeus. This is the encounter.

Some people will say, "Jesus never changed his mind!" But this simply does not make sense. Jesus, "like us in all things but sin," has to be affected by other people's need;

otherwise, he would be lacking in compassion, impervious to the cries of the poor, and therefore not the Son of God! So they were leaving Jericho with his disciples. And just note how these disciples are behaving: because it's like a crowd of what we call in England "Yobbos," or worse. You can tell immediately that the disciples are not exactly sophisticated or genteel people. And they will come more directly into this story in just a moment. But Jesus, and his disciples, and a great multitude, are moving forward. Meanwhile, Bartimaeus, the blind beggar, son of Timaeus, is sitting by the roadside.

Notice first, the rather curious fact that this beggar is actually given a name. In this way, he is raised up to the dignity of a "somebody," a person with an identity. The rich man doesn't have a name, but this poor man does! We remember the promise about the poor being exalted, and the rich laid low. So Bartimaeus is given a name, and thus a context. He's called "the son of Timaeus" and he's given a history, however minimal: He belongs somewhere; he is somebody's son. And now he's sitting by the roadside and something momentous is about to happen. You can just tell; it's in the air.

Now we have to use our imagination, and this is important. We have Jesus, surrounded by a crowd of people on the road. The road is not an eight-lane highway; the "road" is not much more than a track. There's a multitude of people on the road itself, and at the sides of the road. Beyond the crowd is Bartimaeus, sitting down. So Bartimaeus couldn't see Jesus even if he wasn't blind. And this is not his only problem: His real problem is that he won't be able to make Jesus hear him even if he shouts, because there's just too much noise, and encounters require a certain quietness. So Bartimaeus is sitting by the roadside, and Mark says a very important thing in the next sentence: "When he *heard* that it was Jesus of Nazareth." There you have it: his humanity comes right through. He's hearing, he's listening, he's attentive and absorbing—he's human!

If you look at some of the great medieval paintings of the Annunciation, Mary is kneeling piously, and in the upper left-hand corner of the painting, you will see a dove fluttering there. Of course, this represents the Holy Spirit. Now and then, not only will you see radiating from the dove seven shafts of light (identified as the seven gifts of the Holy Spirit) but, occasionally, if you take the very center ray of light and extend it with a ruler, it goes straight into Mary's right ear! The symbolism is very clear: not only that "she conceived by the Holy Spirit" but that she received *the Word* into her ear, through her attentive listening! We are used to talking about the virgin birth, and this is an imaginative—but profoundly significant and human—representation of how she became pregnant. She received the Word and nurtured it until she was able to bring it to birth. Another curiosity is that in many languages, the verb "to speak" is exactly the same as the verb "to give birth"! So Mary brought forth, uttered, gave birth to the living word! The medieval iconographers and painters were aware of this sense that Mary gestated the word and gave it birth. In the context of a community that identified the notion of humanity, of being human, in terms of having ears and listening, this was a very important thing.

Mark has almost hidden this little gem. Bartimaeus *heard* that it was Jesus; he recognized Jesus, if you like, by sound, by careful listening. But now Bartimaeus is in a bit of a quandary. There's not very much he can do, given his position. But if he doesn't succeed in what he wants to do, he's never going to get the chance again! So will he risk everything, or will he let a golden opportunity slip away? Is the situation hopeless? How many times in our own life do we think that Jesus might be passing by, but we can't get his attention? What's the point? Me? I can't do anything. So we just sit there and do nothing—and sometimes complain anyway! But Bartimaeus has real courage. He's actually very cunning. Let's look at what he does.

First, imagine you are in a shopping mall on a Saturday afternoon, and there are thousands of people around making an enormous hubbub. Imagine, for example, that your name is Julie. And suddenly you hear someone shouting "Julie!" You can't help yourself; you instinctively respond to it! Just for a fraction of a second, you might wonder if it's you whose name is being called—but it's too late; you've already turned around! There is in all of our lives the embarrassment of turning around and discovering that it was some other "Julie." It wasn't us at all! So now what does Bartimaeus do? He yells out, but the very first word he yells is "Jesus!"

Jesus is passing by. Jesus is busy. The crowd is noisy. But he hears his name! Instinctively, he hesitates, or stops. It's enough for Bartimaeus, who immediately follows it up with "Son of David!" Now this is the first step of Bartimaeus' coming to faith, naming Jesus, and identifying him by a title. "Jesus, Son of David," he shouts. First of all, it may seem rather impertinent, because there is no indication the two have met, and here's Bartimaeus addressing Jesus by his first name! Who does he think he is? Evidently, that's how the disciples respond. So Bartimaeus is taking quite a risk by "taking" Jesus' first name, when he hasn't been "given" it first. Then he calls Jesus "Son of David." This is astonishing: It's a messianic title, a name that people in the crowd would find shocking. This is an act of faith for Bartimaeus. This is a statement out of the profundity of this man's being. You don't just go around calling people "Son of David." There is an insight, there is a depth of perception, and it will be revealed very clearly in just a few moments.

This first identification of Jesus then, is already a massive stride along the road to faith. But Bartimaeus isn't finished. He shouts again, "Jesus, Son of David, have mercy on me!" To ask for mercy is to identify not simply the Son of David in a general way, but to identify somebody who has the capacity to have mercy, somebody who has the capacity to have God's mercy, and somebody who has the capacity to respond to a "nobody," a blind beggar! So it's hardly surprising that "many rebuked him, telling him to be silent." This is the closing of ranks, the disciples "looking after" Jesus and doing some crowd management! Here's the institution protecting its celebrity, its important personage. Here we see the disciples flexing their muscles, using their petty power to control the blind man. "Many rebuked him, telling him to be silent." It was as if they were saying, "Who do you think you are, calling on Jesus?" They were putting him in his place, presuming to have authority to do so, and assuming that Jesus would endorse them. Who are the people who rebuked him? The disciples! The apostles! The self-appointed "minders"!

"Many rebuked him, telling him to be silent. But he cried out all the more." What determination! What courage! Here's faith again. The establishment, the pillars of the establishment are telling you to be quiet, but your voice rises—not in indignation but in faith! So Bartimaeus "cried out all the more, crying 'Son of David, have mercy on me!' " He doesn't need to address him by name anymore, because he has Jesus' attention. And he doesn't need to be impertinent. So he focuses now very closely on this naming of Jesus: "Son of David, have mercy on *me*!" He's saying, "You're all I've got; don't let me down; please, please, God, help me!" Bartimaeus is really, really committing himself in faith.

The next sentence is: "And Jesus stopped." It's astonishingly abrupt and very dramatic."Jesus stopped." Then he said, "Call him!" The focus, the immediacy quite breathtaking:

Jesus stopped and issued the call. It's going to come through a third party, because Jesus cannot see Bartimaeus, who is hidden by the crowds. And, of course, Bartimaeus can't see Jesus because he's blind!

This call will be pivotal for Bartimaeus, and it will turn into a commission. And the very people who, only a moment before, had said, "Shut up, you godless beggar" (or words to that effect), are now the very people to call the blind man, saying, "Take heart, rise, he is calling you." How two-faced! How hypocritical! These are chameleons, fair-weather friends, weather-cocks, fickle and superficial. And *they* are the disciples, people who should know better, people who actually think they do know better: They think they are superior but they are certainly "of little faith," indeed, compared to blind Bartimaeus.

One minute they're saying "No, keep away!" and then, as soon as Jesus indicates his interest, they're saying so obsequiously, "Yes, please come!" Now the phrase Mark gives them—"Take heart"—is a very good phrase word for us to ponder. Take *heart* has the same root as courage, or encourage: The word *cor,* or *coeur* (en-cour-age), means "have heart, have a heart, be hearty." Jesus is saying to him, have courage, but he is also saying to him, "*take* courage: have *my* courage: I'll be your courage." This is truly an encounter. Ironically, it's the disciples who put it into words, though they can hardly grasp the significance of what they are saying: "Have courage. Rise. He is calling you."

Now, we are getting to the most dramatic moment of the encounter. Recall that Bartimaeus is blind. He's being called to go to Jesus. But the only way he knows where Jesus is, is by the words that Jesus has said a moment before, which are "Call him." He's only heard Jesus say *two words,* and he's got to find out exactly where Jesus is, just by sound. People are saying "Take heart, rise, he is calling you." Now he is going to have to make this jump, from where he is to where Jesus is, with nothing but sound to help him! It's truly a do-or-die moment! He *must* make it to Jesus. If he doesn't make it, he's missed his one and only chance. He knows he can do it; but there's one potential problem, one inhibiting factor—and that is his cloak. If he tries to get up and jump to Jesus but trips and stumbles over his cloak, he'll be flat on his face! He will *not* be able to come to Jesus, however much he wants to! What will he do?

The book of Exodus (22:26–27) says this: "If you take your neighbor's cloak in pawn, you shall restore it before the sun goes down; for it may be your neighbor's only clothing to use as cover; in what else shall that person sleep? And if your neighbor cries out to me, I will listen, for I am compassionate."

What a remarkable passage and promise! Bartimaeus is a poor, poor beggar and under his cloak he is naked. He has nothing. Nothing. Or, to put it differently, all he has is his cloak. And he has just cried out and is being heard by Jesus! Not long before, Jesus had said to the rich man, "Sell all you have, and come." Now Bartimaeus is going to get rid of all he has in order to come. What does he care if he's naked, he's also blind! What does he care if they laugh at him, so long as he gets to Jesus, it won't matter. The only thing that matters now—the *only* thing—is that he makes it to Jesus; he must not trip and fall! So, flinging away his cloak, he comes to Jesus in a leap! It's very, very dramatic. And it's an image, a model if you like, of our own conversion.

There is a cloak in the lives of each of us, something that comes between us and Jesus, between the call and the response. What do we do? Do we bargain with God, saying, "You can't possibly want this"? Do we fail to come to Jesus, just as he is passing by? Do we miss the encounter? Or do we just grab our "cloak" and wrap it even more tightly around ourselves because we're afraid to be seen to be naked, afraid of what people might say, afraid of what they will notice? The message Bartimaeus offers us is quite different: "No, no, no! Don't hold back! Go to the one who calls!" He sprang up, and we know that we can too.

There's a word that occurs very little in the New Testament, but it will recur when Jesus is talking to the woman at the well and says "I will give you living water that will *spring up* to eternal life." And this is exactly what Bartimaeus does: he "springs up" to eternal life! Jesus turns to him and says, "What do you want me to do for you?" Now, if we could believe that Jesus might encounter us in a way that would allow us to hear him asking of us, "Tell me what you need," then maybe we would have the courage to say what we need. What we *need*—not just what we *want*, but what we need. Because Jesus wants to persuade Bartimaeus that their interests can converge, that God really has people's best interests at heart.

Here is a moment of truth for Bartimaeus and for us. How would we respond? How do we respond to the gentle voice of the Christ who asks us to name our deepest needs? So very often we simply identify what we want, which isn't what we need at all, and we never make the distinction between wants and needs. But the blind man says, without a trace of hesitation: "Master" (using the word Mary Magdalene will use when she meets Jesus in the garden after the Resurrection). She says *Rabbouni,* "my master"; this is the same word, "my master." So, before he names his need, Bartimaeus names his master, and it is the final movement to faith and discipleship, because of the word "my." Bartimaeus has moved from "Jesus, Son of David" to "Son of David, have mercy," to "my master." "My master," he says, "you are the center of my life." Now he says, "Let me see," and in some translations, "Let me receive my sight." But the word actually means let me see *again*. Because Bartimaeus was not always blind. Bartimaeus could see once. Bartimaeus has a memory of being able to see! When Jesus says, "What do you want me to do for you?" Bartimaeus is asking for *restoration,* but restoration in a very biblical sense: not just restoration to the *status quo ante* (the way things once were), but restoration in the sense of *renewal:* a kind of "make-over," a deeper or more profound experience of humanness. What Bartimaeus gets *superficially* is restored sight; but what he gets at a much deeper level is *insight* or *perception*—not just *vision*. He gets the insight of faith. This is what he had asked for: "Deepen my sight. Deepen my sight. Restore it so that I will recognize my God passing by."

Jesus says to him, "Go your way." Now you can see the pattern as it finally unfolds: "Come; Go; Go your way." But now Bartimaeus' way is Jesus' way. Jesus left Bartimaeus to choose it. "Go your way. Your faith has made you well." His faith made him well! Miracles don't make faith; it is faith that makes miracles. And here's one of the finest examples in the New Testament: "Your faith has made you well." Jesus is not taking any credit for this. Jesus is saying, "I'm the facilitator of your encounter and your journey to faith, and this is what has restored you."

Then Mark uses a word he uses frequently: the word is "immediately." You find it, for example, when Peter is sinking under the waves and he cries out—*immediately* Jesus is there, reaching out to save him. Mark wants to say there is no gap between your need and Jesus' response. You may think there is, you may feel there is, but that may be because of your lack of faith, because of your unwillingness to rely on God or to trust in God. So, "immediately he received his sight and followed him along the way." The restoration is instantaneous. The discipleship, the following, is also instantaneous!

With his faith affirmed, Bartimaeus leaves *his* way once and for all. He leaves his life at the *wayside* and follows Jesus, by moving from the *wayside*, from being *by the way*, on to the main road, the *highway*. He follows Jesus, (who is *The* Way) on *The Way*. There, he did it! And look at him: He was just a nobody, a poor old blind beggar!

Applications

It's important not simply to use our imagination to get a clearer picture of what these stories are portraying, but to apply them to our lives in order to encounter Jesus and come to discipleship ourselves.

Look for the stages as a person comes to faith. Sometimes it happens almost instantaneously, and sometimes it takes two or three steps. Sometimes it's easier for us to identify with the people who come slowly to faith. So we can examine how they get onto the road or onto the *Way* of Jesus. We can look at how they are called in order to be sent, so that the sending becomes the fulfillment of the calling. We, too, are not only called, but called to be sent.

Then ask yourself how you can make the connections in your own life, by looking at the details in particular stories. Remember the woman in Luke's story. She has been bent over for eighteen years. She's been bent over so much that she can only see the floor; she can't even look up, or around her. She cannot see the walls, she cannot see the sky, she cannot see the trees, because she's been bent over for eighteen years. Eighteen years ago was in the mid-eighties. How many of us have been bent over in some way for years—perhaps since the mid-eighties, or even before? And what are we, or the church of God or Christ, doing about it? If we bring these gospel stories into our lives, they might help us to formulate questions that are important for our faith development. The

stories offer us a way to encounter Jesus and to be encountered by Jesus. Not only could they change our lives—if the
serve both to call us and to send us—they might even change
the world.

Let us have the courage to come to the God who calls, to
ask God to disturb our lives, to trust the God who disturbs,
and to go in God's name to disturb the world!

For Reflection

◈ Which one story about Jesus is most compelling in your
own spiritual journey? Retell that story now.

◈ If you were to compare the life of your parish to the life of
Jesus, which stories of the Gospel most describe how your
parish operates?

◈ Jesus encountered many characters during his brief but
intense years of ministry. In your town or neighborhood,
with which characters would Jesus have been most likely to
spend time?

Maureen Shaughnessy

A Quiet Revolution
Taking Place

THE RECENT EVENTS OF THE CHURCH OVER THE
last several years, dealing with the sexual abuse scandal, the
resignation of Cardinal Law, and the changing face of the
United States hierarchy as many bishops reach retirement age,
all highlight the need for dialogue, communication, and
bridge building if we are to be a vibrant faith-filled faith
community.

The changes in society continue to challenge us daily—the
uncertainty about war, the daily violent struggles in the
Mideast, the evident downsides of globalization, the
confrontation with other nations—never mind the serious
economic struggles here in our own country—challenge us as
a faith community in significant ways. The tragedy of the
Columbia space shuttle is another sobering reality.

A quiet revolution is taking place. The church in the United States, even before the events mentioned above but more so now, is realizing that if faith is truly to be alive and vibrant then adults must be taken seriously and their faith lives nurtured, challenged, and formed. I like to think that part of this is due to the issuance of the U.S. bishops' pastoral plan for adult faith formation, *Our Hearts Were Burning Within Us* in 1999. I think in some ways it might be likened to a tipping point—if any of you are familiar with the writings of Malcom Gladwell—how little things make a big difference. He suggests that there is a certain point at which things happen.

Certainly before 1999, there were many successful and hopeful signs that adult faith formation was being done. In fact, I would say from my experience that adult faith formation has been a serious effort in the U.S. church since Vatican II, but some of the difficulty in rooting it in our parishes has been because the emphasis has been on programs and not on an overall, compelling vision of what adult faith formation is about. I think *Our Hearts Were Burning Within Us* has made a significant contribution to the visioning, building on what was presented in both the *Catechism of the Catholic Church* and in the *General Directory for Catechesis*. We need to reorient our understanding of formation within our parishes/faith communities toward helping adults see the need for their own faith formation rather than focusing on children and youth.

When you survey the terrain since Vatican II, you can see the peaks and valleys of what has happened in adult faith formation. Many dioceses after Vatican II established positions in offices of religious education that had primary responsibility for adult faith formation—I started there myself. Many dioceses in the late 1970s and early 1980s began to develop renewal programs for parishes that were primarily targeted at adults—*Christ Renews His Parish*,

Renew, and more recently *Disciples in Mission.* Scripture study programs developed and are still going strong today. Parent programs, especially for those whose children were preparing for reception of sacraments, were certainly prevalent and still are today. Many were successful and served as evangelizing opportunities.

Many dioceses began efforts in social concerns, in evangelization and in catechist and lay ministry programs—all to the good, but often not seen as part of a whole but rather individual efforts. It is the big picture that is needed if we are to move forward. If our hearts are truly burning, we need to fan the fire—to stir it up 'til it is a mighty blaze! The vision offered in the pastoral is one of discipleship, that both as individual believers and as members of the church we understand ourselves to be persons on a lifelong journey, which demands ongoing formation so that we might be what we are called to be by virtue of our baptism—disciples of Jesus Christ, continuing his mission. We need a formation that nurtures a profound, lifelong conversion, a formation that opens adults to grow in the life of Christ through experience, reflection, prayer, and study

The bishops say there are two outcomes they hope to have happen as a result of implementing the plan:

We seek to form parishes that are vitally alive in faith. These communities will provide a parish climate and an array of activities and resources designed to help adults more fully understand and live their faith.

We seek to form adults who actively cultivate a lively baptismal and eucharistic spirituality with a powerful sense of mission and apostolate. Nourished by word, sacrament, and communal life, they will witness and share the Gospel in their homes, neighborhoods, places of work, and centers of culture.

This offers us a vision of forming communities of disciples—people who know and appreciate the gift that has been given to them in baptism—the gift of life in God.

These two goals really speak to what I would like to identify as the five Cs of adult faith formation and which indicate areas that we need to give attention to if we want adult faith formation to be rooted in our parishes and dioceses: Conversion, Call to Discipleship, Culture, Curriculum, and Christian Community.

Conversion

We need to recognize that many adults don't really understand their faith in ways that truly touch their everyday lives. We need to invite adults to be open to the Lord. Our parishes need to be gathering places where people find opportunities to worship, certainly, but beyond that parishes need to provide multiple opportunities for people to engage in dialogue about the things that matter and to create forums that foster sustained conversations. As leaders we need to become companions on the journey who are attentive to the stories and needs of those we accompany. Keeping in mind the gospel story of Luke about the two disciples on the road to Emmaus, we realize that we are privileged to share and live faith with others

Call to Discipleship

Our invitation to our adults asks them to accept the challenge of being nourished by the word of God and Eucharist so that they too might have the experience of the disciples: of recognizing the Lord, having their hearts burn within them, and be moved to share the good news with others. It is, as the GDC says, to make faith living, articulate, and fruitful in the lives of believers (82).

Culture

We live in a diverse multicultural society; pluralism is the norm in our world. According to any number of surveys (both scientific and popular) there is a widespread spiritual hunger in our people. (If you aren't convinced of that, look to the ever-expanding sections on spirituality in a Barnes & Noble or a Borders bookstore.) It is a world being reshaped by ever-new forms of technology and the increasing globalization of society with both their positive and negative consequences. The events of 9/11, the increasing march toward war as a solution to international conflict or terrorism, and the confrontation with North Korea challenge us every day to examine our real values as a nation and to reflect on how we see ourselves in relationship to the rest of the world. To put it rather vividly, Thomas Hawkins says in his book *The Learning Congregation* that we are "white-water rafting through the rapids of social, technological, and demographic change" (p.3).

Curriculum

I want to mention this fourth C briefly and then refer you to the Leader's Guide for *Our Hearts Were Burning Within Us* for greater detail. The *General Directory for Catechesis* states: "The maturation of the Christian life requires that it be culti-vated in all its dimensions: knowledge of the faith, liturgical life, moral formation, prayer, belonging to community, missionary spirit. When catechesis omits one of these elements, the Christian faith does not attain full develop-ment" (87). Every dimension of parish life opens us to catechetical opportunities, if we would just open our eyes. Think of it as a web that encompasses the whole and weaves connections of the parts one to the other. The pastoral plan suggests a wide number of possible themes, activities, skills development, etc., that are derived from the six tasks of cate-chesis—proclaiming the message, liturgical education, moral formation, prayer, education for community life, and missionary initiative. Let me cite a few examples: Under "knowledge of the faith": "explore the Scriptures so that adults may be hearers and doers of the word." "Learn the richness of the Church's tradition . . ." (91). Under "liturgical life": "acquire the spirituality, skills, and habits of full, conscious, and active participation in the liturgy, especially the Eucharistic liturgy" (92). And so forth—you get the idea !

It would be hard to exhaust the possibilities—it is such an inclusive and comprehensive way to approach the develop-ment of intentional opportunities within a parish, region, or diocese.

I want to also mention under this the growing interest in developing intergenerational programs that are built around the liturgical year—Kathleen Chesto's *FIRE* program has been used for a good while now. Another that is currently being used in some twenty dioceses, and another twenty will begin this year, is the approach created by John Roberto of the Center for Ministry Development called *Generations of Faith*. It is also the approach called for by Bill Huebsch in his book *Whole Community Catechesis*.

Community

This encompasses the parish in every dimension of its life forms, its members in a living faith—through proclamation, teaching, worship, service, and community life. The quality of life within a faith community—within a parish—is crucial for effective faith formation. For most Catholics, the parish is the single most important aspect of the church. The *General Directory for Catechesis* strongly and explicitly speaks to the central role of a parish in faith formation. Its says: "The

Christian community is the origin, locus and goal of catechesis" (254); "the parish is, without doubt, the most important locus in which the Christian community is formed and expressed. . . . It constitutes . . . a very adequate community space for the realization of the ministry of the word at once as teaching, education and life experience. . . . It must continue to be . . . the prime mover and preeminent place for catechesis" (257). The call for renewed attention to adult faith formation is not primarily about establishing new programs but about gaining a new perspective on the parish as a learning community. A learning community is one where some or all of the following conditions exist:

1. Individuals are always growing, learning, changing;
2. people are willing to examine both their own assumptions and those of others;
3. people express mutual respect for other people;
4. there is an openness to experimentation and a recognition that failure is possible—willingness to risk;
5. the whole community is continually expanding its capacity to create its future. (Hawkins, p.144).

Our parishes need to be true learning communities— concerned for what really matters.

The pastoral plan offered three goals for why we should be doing adult faith formation and all three have to do with the five Cs mentioned above. First, "to acquire an attitude of conversion to the Lord." Our baptism gifts us; it places us in a relationship with God and with the community of faith, one which we need to nourish and develop. As Catholics, we believe this happens best in and through the experience of a believing community. It reminds us of our dependence on God, our sinfulness—our need for repentance and reconciliation. We are called to holiness—to wholeness.

The second goal is to help us as adults make "a conscious and firm decision to live the gift and choice of faith through membership in the Christian community accepting co-responsibility for the community's mission and internal life." This is not about membership in an association, prestigious club, or organization—it's not enough to declare oneself Catholic on a form or in a census. It is about being committed disciples, consciously and responsibly choosing to live the way of life we are called to by baptism, to embrace the teachings of Jesus, and to be transformed and to witness to this in our homes, neighborhoods, workplaces, society.

The third goal is to help us as adults be equipped to act as disciples in mission to the world. Our faith is not only about personal holiness; we are called to transform the social and temporal order, a dual calling to evangelization and justice. We are about building the reign of God. Our attitudes, values, and practices must demonstrate our faith in every dimension of our lives. It takes courage to live a Christian lifestyle in our society today.

As you reflect on these goals, what do you believe is a major challenge for you and/or your parish with respect to them? Do they suggest entry points for you of what we might do for adult faith formation?

This period of time is one of new vitality and challenge for the church, a period in which adult Catholic laity will play a pivotal leadership role in fulfilling the mission of evangelizing and transforming society. If there ever was a time that calls for this it is now. The past few years have been a time of great pain for all of us who are a part of this church. I suspect there is not a diocese untouched by the sexual abuse scandals, the financial situations that arise from this, and the direct effect this has on the ability of dioceses and parishes to provide the pastoral ministries needed by the People of God. The questioning and mistrust of leadership in the church—especially the bishops—continues to challenge all of us, whatever role we play.

The media coverage has not stopped and at times has been overwhelming. We are challenged to our very roots to name that which we really value. The "isms" of our day—racism, sexism, secularism, materialism—affect us consciously and unconsciously in our daily choices, actions, and inactions. The seeming indifference of church members, those who become disillusioned and who leave, those who treat their role in church as a club membership that gives them rights and privileges while neglecting to take seriously their responsibilities and obligations, are concerns as we try to minister effectively to the diverse populations in our faith communities. For our faith communities to come alive, to burn with love of God and of neighbor, to burn with love of God and of neighbor, the church needs a laity that is educated, articulate, and willing to speak the truth in love. It is risky but necessary. It is in the everyday that faith is challenged.

The plan very practically suggests that for all of this to happen there must be an infrastructure created within the parish. It is described in terms of four roles:

The pastor and all other pastoral staff members— the parish staff needs to explicitly support and provide the resources to create viable adult faith formation in the parish—they need to be models themselves of lifelong learning.

The adult faith formation leader—the parish needs to have someone identified as responsible for teaching adult faith formation in the parish. It can be a staff member, full or part-time, or a volunteer. The critical criterion is that the person be competent for the position.

The adult faith formation team—this will take different forms from parish to parish, but a group of four to eight people is needed who will work to design and implement intentional faith formation opportunities for adults and who will network with all other committees or groups in the parish as appropriate. We are presently surveying dioceses to see what is already happening with regard to the training of such teams and will publish the results to our diocesan contacts so that they can benefit from what is already being done. We don't need to reinvent the wheel. We are also talking with one of the major publishers about creating a video-assisted program similar to Priming the Pump, which some of you may remember, and a video on "methods in adult catechesis" is a future addition to *Echoes of Faith*.

The catechist of adults—this person is adequately prepared to work with adults and knows, understands, and can work with how adults learn. Several dioceses now provide a certification for this role. Again, we are gathering the information so that we can share what is happening.

The vision for adult faith formation is one of collaborative ministry. It is a weaving of different aspects of parish life into a whole, taking advantage of the multiple openings for challenging one another to growth in faith.

Since the issuance of the plan in 1999, several resources have been available to assist people:

St. Anthony Messenger Press published a *Catholic Update Video, On Fire With Faith: Forming Adult Disciples.* In collaboration with RCL, the United States Catholic Conference produced the video-assisted program *Seeds of Promise, Seeds of*

Faith, which gives the foundational themes of the *General Directory for Catechesis* and *Our Hearts Were Burning Within Us.* In November, 2002 we sent to every diocesan bishop a copy of a workshop designed for clergy education entitled "Cultivating the Word." Many publishers have produced materials that are certainly supportive of the vision of the plan. We need to get the word out.

NACARE, the National Advisory Committee for Adult Religious Education, which serves the Department of Education, asked some key questions of dioceses about implementation of the plan in its survey in the winter of 2000. This is what they discovered:

93 dioceses responded;

16 dioceses told us that they had added, or had budgeted to add, a staff person;

22 had revised job descriptions for existing staff persons;

38 had begun advisory boards;

9 revised responsibilities of existing boards;

42 had done staff inservices;

63 had offered workshops to parish staffs, committees and other groups;

most dioceses responded that they felt about 30 percent of their parishes had implemented efforts in adult faith formation.

About the same time, the Office of Family, Laity, Women and Youth did an electronic survey of Catholic adults on their parishes and their needs and received over 59,000 responses. By far and away the area cited as of greatest need and interest was adult faith formation. Now you can imagine the range this represented, but still people identified adult faith formation as an area of great concern for them.

So much is happening! So much is already under way. Each of you must do what is most appropriate in your setting. The plan suggests that you . . .

- study the plan as parish staff and parish council/committee;

- assess your particular situation;

- determine what is going on in your parish, diocese, civil community;

- pay attention to the local issues in your communities;
- make up a list of the resources available to you and begin to consider options:

    —What are already existing priorities in the parish that need to be connected to this effort?

    —Develop action steps—goals, objectives, strategies.

    —Attend to the various relational networks and populations within your parish.

    —Prepare your leaders—identify, invite, train, and support those adults who will be involved.

    —Above all, recognize that this will take lots of time!

Leaders need to be prepared. Identify, invite, train, and support those adults who will have any role in creating a viable adult faith formation effort in your parish.

Keep the fires burning within you. Know that the end is not to put on programs or events, but to share the Good News of God's overwhelming love for us revealed in the person of Jesus Christ.

Let me quote the concluding paragraph of our bishops' pastoral:

> Awakened and energized by the Spirit, let us strengthen our commitment and intensify our efforts to help adults in our communities be touched and transformed by the life-giving message of Jesus, to explore its meaning, experience its power, and live in its light as faithful adult disciples today. Let us do our part with creativity and vigor, our hearts aflame with love to empower adults to know and live the message of Jesus. This is the Lord's work. In the power of the Spirit it will not fail but will bear lasting fruit forth life of the world (183).

So let us not procrastinate. I remember when I first went into diocesan ministry. I discovered a small book on adult religious education by a pastor from the Midwest, whose name I believe was Father McGrath. He related the following story: The planning committee had its first meeting and they began to look at the calendar to determine when they would offer certain programs and events. They decided to skip the fall because so many other things were starting up and they didn't want to compete for the attention of the adults. One of the members noted that they certainly couldn't plan on doing much in the winter, given the unpredictable weather. Several noted that spring is filled with so many family celebrations and, of course, they all agreed that summer is vacation time.

So what does that leave us with? Do we believe that adult faith formation is something that is part of all seasons and essential? Or do we think of it as an add-on, something nice to offer whenever possible? Our own stance will determine our commitment to furthering this ministry. Will you fan the fire or let it die out? The choice is yours.

For Reflection

❖ What is the most important source of adult education about the Church and the Gospels for you? Where do you get most of your own information about the faith?

❖ What opportunities are there in the life of your parish for adult formation where people are already gathered? How could you offer more to folks who want it within your parish?

❖ In what ways can your parish speak more clearly about the values and teachings of the Gospel to the community around you? How do you utilize local communications media for that purpose now?

Fran Ferder and John Heagle

Shaping New Wineskins for Our Time: The Future of Human Loving

Fran:

IN THE MONTH OF JANUARY, 2003, JOHN AND I were privileged to do a series of three Wednesday evenings on the subject of sexuality and relationships for students in the campus ministry department at Seattle University. Kelly had been there for all three sessions, attentive and serious. After the third night, she came up to us just as we were packing up and getting ready to go, and she said: "Could I just ask you one quick question about love?"

Well, I know there are no quick questions about love, so we put our briefcases down and we tried to listen to Kelly. She prefaced her question, which was poignant, with a couple of statements: "My parents divorced when I was three. My mother later remarried and divorced again. I have an older brother who's gay and he just told me a couple of months ago that he's leaving the Catholic Church because he doesn't think he can live without an experiential love relationship his whole life."

Then she said: "My roommate and I are really considering whether or not we should have children because of the threats of terrorism, suicide bombers, talk of war—all of those things. We really are concerned." She was very serious. Her brown eyes got very wide and she poised herself to ask what may be *the* question for her generation: "Given all that, what do you think my chances are for living in a world and in a church where love is stronger than fear or hatred?"

It's a powerful question, isn't it? Kelly was asking: "For people in my generation, does love have a future?" Kelly is familiar with what we call the crisis of sexuality. She is familiar with it in her own life. She is familiar with it on an interpersonal level in her neighborhood. She hears of it all the time on a global level. She knows that relationships are breaking down at all levels. She knows too about the crisis of sexual abuse in the church—she had talked to us the week before about her cousin, who had been abused by a priest. So she has experienced the crisis of sexuality in her own life, as all of us have.

We don't need to belabor that crisis. We know it's there. Yet we remain people of hope in spite of the fact that sex in our culture is commonly reduced to genital behavior, and not only in our society, but also in the church. Sex, sexuality, and human loving are exploited by the media. Sex is often viewed less as an experience of mutuality and intimacy and just as frequently as one more opportunity for recreation, outside of the context of meaningful relationships. How do we as believers, as people of faith, people of hope, and people of imagination, imagine a situation, a church, that has a newer understanding of human sexuality?

John:

We might assume that since the culture doesn't give us a very healthy or holistic or holy dimension of human sexuality that the church would be the logical place to look for this image, this vision, this tradition. We know today that, unfortunately, this is not necessarily the case because of the obvious reason that our churches, and particularly the Roman Catholic Church, are going through a serious crisis of credibility.

Our ability right now to speak on the meaning and ethical values around sexuality has been seriously compromised because of the current sexual abuse crisis among the clergy and its impact everywhere. You know that experience; I know that experience. But at the same time, and this is part of our imagination, we must recognize that when the Judeo-Christian tradition speaks from its best side, when we speak from our deepest and most primal roots in the biblical vision, in the ministry and teaching of Jesus, there isn't a more positive and affirming tradition that speaks about the dignity of human beings, the sacredness of relationships, the radical goodness of the human body, and the giftedness of human sexuality.

The problem, of course, is that we haven't always spoken from our best side. In fact, there is a lingering kind of dualism that takes on many different forms and names. It is sometimes called *docetism*. This is the first heresy the church had to struggle with, right at the time of the New Testament. In the First Letter of John we read, "The word that we speak to you is a word that we have seen with our eyes, touched with our hands and spoken to and been close to and seen as real, the word of life." The Johannine tradition is encountering the earliest and most persistent heresy, the denial not of the divinity of Christ—that's probably the most dramatic heresy—but of Christ's humanity, and therefore the denial of human experience, of human values. It is with this lingering docetism, whether it be Albigensianism or Jansenism or, more closely to our own times, that fundamental claim that spirit is more important than flesh, that souls are far, far more valuable than bodies, where that split, that tendency to compartmentalize, becomes the problem.

The difficulty underlying this I would call the fear of *eros,* the fear of our sexual passions, the fear of desire. This, we believe, is the core crisis not only in our culture but also in our church. In our culture we tend to be so afraid of eros in terms of integrating it that we fuse with it, we become addicted only to the first level of eros, its most primal energy, its instinctive energy. The church in its tradition and all its dualisms is equally afraid of eros, equally afraid of sexual passion, and, I suppose, in all honesty there's probably good reason. Sexual struggles in my own life, trying to integrate my own sexuality, have been a lifelong struggle. I believe it's the same for most people. None of us does this perfectly. None of us has followed a smooth path. We can't foreclose on the struggle—do not pass go, do not pick up your $200, go directly to maturity—we all have to find our way there.

In some ways, it's understandable that we would struggle with eros. But here's how we would view the fundamental Christian struggle—and this is a key part. In the Christian tradition there has been a tendency to hierarchicalize love. We want to be very clear at the beginning that we do not like this. We present this not as something that's attractive but as a difficulty, a spiritual way of skewing the tradition, and it is so pervasive that you will recognize it immediately. Let me give you some examples.

First of all, *agapic* love, *philia,* and *eros* line up like this: agapic love is wonderful and good, philia is okay, but eros is bad. This is the simple, short version. Recently in Seattle, Avery Dulles came to give a presentation to a large group of people. He said it was a severe mistake in the Catholic Church over the last thirty years to begin to say that marriage and celibacy are both equally valid; then he said that celibacy always has been and is a higher way of spiritual living. When I read that in the paper, I said to myself, "I thought we were past this. I thought we were over this kind of hierarchicalization." This is the leftover dualism; it's alive and well and it's all around us; its whole approach is that the agapic love that comes from God is fine and it's the only kind of love we should all attend to.

I'm all for agapic loving. Philia is also very acceptable. This is the mutual love of friendship. Then there's this great gap that exists between these two forms of love and eros—it's almost like eros gets demonized. This is a strong word, but it does get stigmatized, and it becomes a problem for all of us because of the attention we tend to give to that. When eros is demonized or looked down upon, or somehow compartmentalized, it is expressed in very unhealthy ways. We repress it or become addicted to an unhealthy eros that's not integrated. How do we get away from hierarchicalizing love and try to re-imagine and reclaim an integrating perspective on human sexuality, where eros is the primal energy, the fire at the very core of our lives?

We both believe that we're all called ultimately to agapic compassion. Compassion is the greatest form of agapic love. But you can't be compassionate if you are not passionate. You might be benevolent and you might even be nice, but we don't need benevolent, nice people. We need passionate people, prophets. We need people who love and who love from this dimension of their lives, from the erotic fire and energy of their own being. The Buddhists have a beautiful way of putting this. The Buddhist proverb says that sex is the seed, love is the flower, compassion is the fragrance. This is a very simple way of expressing what we are trying to discuss. How do we recover the importance of the seed? And I'm not just talking here about sperm. I'm talking about that primal energy that all of us experience, whether we are women or men.

The greatest task today in the church is to try to integrate eros, a way not of compartmentalizing eros but bringing it back and reclaiming it, affirming it, celebrating it so that there can be erotic justice and erotic relationships and erotic compassion. I'm using the word *erotic* here, obviously, not in the way our popular culture uses it. But we need to use the word eros because we need to reclaim it. It's unfortunate that in translations of the New Testament and even in the original Greek that the word *eros* is never used, only *philia* and *agape*, because eros was already identified with the Greek, Corinthian notion of a compartmentalized, dionysiac, instinctive experience of sexuality. The task for each of us is how we reclaim this sexual energy, and the task of all of us as a community is how we do the same in a communal relationship.

Let me be very clear about this. About twenty-five years ago when Fran and I began working together, we gave a presentation that I still remember well. We stated that the issue of sexuality is going to be the issue that will make or break the Roman Catholic Church. I would say that this statement is as relevant and as vital and as challenging today. The issue of reclaiming our human sexuality will either make us or break us. So what is this energy and how can we understand it?

Fran:

In re-imaging this notion of human sexuality, you will notice that John and I titled this chapter "The Future of Human Loving" and then began our reflections on sexuality. The reason for this is because they are so profoundly integrated. In re-imaging sexuality we need to move beyond the tendency of our culture and church to narrow sexuality to genital behavior only. Our churches give us rules for genital restraint and our culture titillates us with genital excitement. We too rarely connect sexuality and spirituality; we too rarely connect sexuality and human loving. We certainly see loving expressions of sexuality as holy in the context of human lovemaking, when there's mutuality and tenderness and caring—all those things that make something sacramental.

But we also experience our sexuality in so many other ways. We describe sexuality primarily as energy for relationship, an energy that is built into our DNA, into every fiber of our being. We cannot give it up. We cannot fast from our sexual energy. We cannot enter into a lifetime of not experiencing it or not feeling it. We would be dead inside and certainly not compassionate. There are so many ways to express it, but I want to use just one example.

We like to think of sexuality in a broad sense as inherently eucharistic, as an invitation into communion. We know that the Eucharist is a sacrament; traditionally, we understand that we receive the body of Christ in the sacrament of Eucharist. Too often, however, this understanding has been an isolated, privatized, me-and-Jesus kind of experience. The Eucharist is both the reception of the body of Christ and also an experience of becoming the body of Christ. It's metaphor as well as reality. Who is, after all, the body of Christ? We are. So how do we receive one another? This is the big question of Eucharist. Not just some of us, not just those of us who keep the rules and live by the correct statements or never make any sexual mistakes, but all of us. How do we both receive the body of Christ and be the body of Christ? This question is huge and important to re-imagine when we look at the whole issue of human sexuality. It's so much more than what we do or don't do with our genitals. It's what we do or don't do with our hearts.

Part of re-imaging and re-understanding sexuality links us to the emerging cosmic story. We know, for example, that there are so many kinds of energy in the universe. We had an experience just a matter of months ago of an image of energy that shook all of us to our foundations. Imagine being in a space capsule that is heated on the outside to 3,000 degrees as it reenters the earth's atmosphere. Energy is hot; it's not cold. Human passion is hot. Coldness in relationships, distance, apathy, judgment are indicators in a person of an absence of passion, an absence of Eucharist on the inside, an inability to be and to receive the body of Christ.

There are many forms of energy in the universe. Brian Swimme has given the term *cosmic allurement* to the form we commonly call gravity. I like cosmic allurement better. Gravity is one of the four primary forms of energy in the universe that causes large bodies and small ones to be attracted to each another. So when that spaceship came close to reentering the earth's atmosphere, the pull was so strong that it literally sucked it in, and this time it couldn't survive the heat. That's energy, isn't it? I can't even imagine energy that powerful with my finite thinking, anything that hot and that strong, but we have to imagine a love that is that hot and that strong and enter into it. We're supposed to be like that. That hot and strong energy of attraction beckons all of us to enter into it. And when that gravity or attraction in the universe becomes conscious and intentional, focused and disciplined and warm in you and me, we call it love. Sexuality is the energy of that attraction that draws us, that compels us, that urges us to move toward one another in all kinds of forms and experiences of human communion.

John

The cosmic story becomes embodied in each one of us. Teilhard de Chardin says that we are the arrow of evolution. Ideally, this means that we will carry it forward. It also means, to the extent that we become intentional and conscious of our own cosmic allurement toward each other, and that we live this out mutually with dignity and respect and reverence, that we are integrating this incredible energy into the experience of Christian community and into loving. All of us—young and old, women and men, gay or straight—all of us have one fundamental, universal vocation. Each one of us is called to be a life-giver and a lover. Each one of us! This means that children are life-givers. We must stop telling children, "Someday you're going to give life." They're already giving life.

We were on a plane going to give a workshop in Los Angeles; we were seated in the back near the bathrooms. When the seatbelt light finally went off and people were in line, right across from us was a three-month-old boy by the name of Ryan, and every time he saw someone coming, his arms and legs would start kicking and he couldn't wait to welcome them. There was all that energy of connection. He had a big smile on his face and everybody got to know Ryan. That was already the beginning. He was already giving life. The question is, and this is an "examination of conscience" question, how are you a life-giver? We want to invite you to claim that, to find words for it.

For you who are parents, who have been married, or who perhaps are grandparents or even great-grandparents, you know the obvious way that you've given life. The church tends to identify life-giver and love with two things, the procreative and the unitive goals of marriage. But what about all you other people? What about you people who are celibate by circumstance? Over half the world today is not married.

How are they lovers and life-givers? What about grandparents after their children have been raised and hopefully launched? Is there life after children? What does it look like? How do you become a generative person then? This is a vital question.

In terms of celibacy, I always thought the greatest issue for me was going to be sexual, physical union with someone else in my life—and it's certainly been a very profound deprivation. What I wasn't anticipating in my mid-forties was another wave of grief that I wasn't going to have children. I had received that as a piece of information, but in my forties it becomes an emotional and experiential reality. So it's very important for me to name how I give life. And I want you to do the same. We want you to name that. Everybody you know in the circle of your relationships is also a lover. They're called to make love, and making love is a lot wider and deeper and more expansive than just having physical intercourse in marriage. That's the liturgy of marriage. But there are lots of other ways in which love is expressed.

In the Hebrew tradition, there are two stories—the priestly story in Genesis, the primal vision, and the Yahwist story—that give us the fundamental priority and mission or the great purpose of sexuality. The first story is filled with all kinds of images of life-giving. Let the seas teem—it's a wonderful expression, "teeming with life." Let the earth grow and bear fruit. All the animals and creatures increase and multiply. This is the phrase we hear again and again. What does it mean for us to "increase and multiply"? Certainly, it means to have children; that's the obvious way. But there are other ways that we are called to increase and to multiply, to deepen the dimensions of our relationship and the dimensions of our experience of community.

The same is true of mutuality, of all forms of friendship. We start already with little children; we say to them "Who's your boyfriend? Who's your girlfriend?" Well, why not say

"Who's your friend?" We start coupling before they're ready to have friendships. The two most missing dimensions of human sexual formation (otherwise known as sex education) are first, formation in communication skills (the most important sexual skill—communication) and second, encouragement in friendship for all levels and experiences of human life.

I want to show you and affirm for you that this is not outside the core of our own contemporary tradition. Look at this wonderful statement from the *Catechism of the Catholic Church*. It's a vision yet to be realized, but I will include it here for you: "Sexuality affects all aspects of the human person in the unity of body and soul. It especially concerns affectivity [that's a large word for emotional experience], the capacity to love and give life and in a more general way the aptitude for forming bonds of communion with others." I probably wouldn't have written it that way, but this is a very profound statement, a statement we ought to live out of.

What if the Catholic Church took this as a mission statement for human sexuality? What are the implications for children, for adolescents, for preparing people for marriage, for gay people in the church community? What would it mean for elderly people who continue to form bonds of communion? Elderly people do not end up not being sexual. Sexuality simply develops. Adulthood is not a terminal state. We all need to claim our human sexuality at another and more profound level. Incarnation is a journey, not an event. In fact, I would even go further than that—and this might sound a little outrageous. I would say that just because you have a body, it doesn't necessarily mean that you are incarnate.

Incarnation means that we embrace our bodiliness, that we enter into the human condition. Many people spend their whole lives looking for the escape hatch from the human condition, for finding the button that says, "I'm out of here."

The two most frequent forms of escape from the human condition around sexuality are repression and addiction. My generation was basically formed in repression. This was our basic model or framework for sexuality, whether you were a seminarian or getting married, or whatever. If you were getting married, sexuality was okay as long as you were going to have it to have children and didn't enjoy it too much. If you were going to be a celibate, it meant going to the fusebox on the wall and taking out the big fuses. You just didn't have any sexual feelings. That was the ideal.

The other form of escaping from incarnation, besides repression, is probably more prominent today—it's called addiction. We get a lot of clients today who are addicted to pornography on the Internet, who are fused with sexual experience at a level that is stuck—the technical word is "fixation"; they can't get beyond that to healthy relationships. Incarnation goes beyond repression, and certainly beyond addiction, to something else. It's called integration. And it takes you along a difficult and very demanding journey. What does it look like?

Fran

It looks like three-month-old Ryan, kicking his legs and smiling broadly when he sees another human face that has eyes that meet his and smile back. It ends for us in this lifetime when we say our final goodbyes to those we love. Remember the recent tragedies. How could any of us forget 9/11, those few people who had cell phones on those planes? What did they want to do? They didn't call their stockbrokers; they wanted more than anything to say one more time, I love you. This is the journey, to learn to say I love you, to learn to be attracted without being fused, to learn to enter into communion relationships that are neither exploitative nor abusive but energizing and life-giving for everyone. This is what the journey means, and it's a long journey. It means to become mature, to grow, to keep growing. This journey doesn't start and end with the beginning and end of puberty. It keeps going. It involves maturing in our capacity to love and give life. The journey never ends.

In the language of psychological or behavioral sciences, this journey is sometimes called "psychosexual development." What we should call it is psychological, emotional, cognitive, informational, social, etc., development, because integration means putting together all the parts of ourselves. It goes through various stages, beginning really before we're even born. We wrote about this in our book *Your Sexual Self: Pathway to Authentic Intimacy* (Ave Maria Press, 1992), which is still available. It outlines this journey from prior to birth where wondrous things are happening inside our mothers' wombs. Remember the words of the psalmist, "You formed me in my mother's womb, a wonder am I."

We are not just growing physically, we are beginning to form responses to emotional cues outside that we hear through the muffled sound of amniotic fluid. We have a startle reflex. Specifically, in the area of psychosexual development, we believe that our sexual orientations are getting their earliest promptings before we are even born. Whether we will be gay or straight or bisexual begins to be influenced prior to birth. Whether we will have a strong or less intense sexual desire. What cues will elicit our sexual responses and our relational interests. All of this is developing even before we're born. Physically or physiologically in the last trimester, little boys are having full or partial erections and little girls are becoming vaginally lubricated. Now you don't need that stuff in utero, but it's so much a part of us. God apparently isn't as dualistic in our creation as sometimes we are ourselves.

How do you integrate these primordial, primitive, sensate responses so that they are directed toward loving and life-giving? Maybe the easiest and quickest way to give a description of this is through a little childhood game that's played in all cultures. It's called peek-a-boo. It's a game that children begin playing as soon as they have a sense of the other and they want to make eye contact. They're beginning to learn some of the most important things about psychosexual development and these are the relational skills for human intimacy and eventual self-disclosure. The baby who's pulling a blanket off its head or peeking out from behind a teddy bear or dad's shoulder to someone who's safe—and they can tell who's safe. You can see me. This is the first voice of psychosexual development or intimacy, the desire to see and be seen.

They're also saying, I'm in charge of my own self-disclosure. You can't take the blanket off my head; I will, and I'll put it back on again when I'm finished showing you my eyes. Children are learning that relating to human beings is pleasurable, or ought to be, and, unless they've been abused or traumatized, they are developing the rudimentary skills for psychosexual development. So the baby who today is saying, You can see my head, will one day be the adult who can say, You can see my dreams. And I don't just have a blanket in front of you, I have words to share with you because I've learned to communicate what's inside my heart and I want you to share it. I want to see your dreams and your stories and your experiences.

This is a brief, nutshell version of what the task of psychosexual development takes us through, the journey to be individuals who can say to one another, I have a lot of passion inside of me and it's directed toward relationships of integrity and of love and of care with everyone, and with some persons much more specially than with others, those "this one at last" moments that are very much a part of that psychosexual development. Who have you said this to? Who have you shared your dreams with, your hopes, your feelings, that affective part of you? This task, as we all know and as John alluded to, requires ongoing conversion.

The spiritual dimension of relational wholeness, or conversion as we call it in our traditional language, can also be described as the development not so much of social skills but of chastity. In other words, instead of looking at psychosexual development from the language of the behavioral scientists, we can look at psychosexual development instead from the language of faith and spirituality. The *Catechism* says that "chastity is a school for the gift of the person." Isn't this an interesting description? A school. School is where we go to learn. In schools we get to make mistakes and nobody excommunicates us. We can go to communion. We learn from our mistakes; we are helped to learn; we are guided and directed because in this school we're learning about what it means to be in communion. Of course, we will make mistakes, so to tell us that we can't have any part of it is simply unthinkable as we re-imagine sexuality and human loving in the future.

I want to emphasize one more thing about chastity and that is that all of us are called to it. Chastity is reverence in relationships. In the first place, chastity is not sexual abstinence. This may be its expression for all of us at one time or another. Married people are called to be chaste in their loving by being reverent toward the person whom they're married to and also by not having sex with anybody else. You can be sexually abstinent inside or outside of marriage, you can abstain from sex with anybody or anybody else, and still not be a chaste person, if you're not reverent in your relationships. We need to re-imagine what chastity calls us to and what it is.

Sexual integration literally means "to come together." It comes from a couple of Latin words, *in* and *tangere,* which mean "to touch into." It means that our knowledge as we grow and develop, our feelings and our experiences, our judgments, our physical desires and urges—and they can be profound at times—our bodily experiences and our values, and all that we couldn't get on this list, all of those things need to touch into each other. What does integration look like? Let's say, for example, that I believe in a vision in which every human person has dignity and therefore must be treated with respect and never used or abused. If I feel attracted to someone and my body tells me I want to have sex with this person, but my knowledge and my judgment and my values also say that I've made a commitment either to celibate chastity or to someone else in marriage, or I don't even know this person's name and I still act with just that one bit of myself, my physical desire, I will not be moving toward psychosexual integration. The more my head and my heart speak to each other, the more I am moving toward greater integration and therefore a greater capacity to be a compassionate person.

There are a number of ways we can know whether we're moving toward integration. There are three signs—not the only three but three that we think are critical (we spell them out in more detail in *Tender Fires: The Spiritual Promise of Sexuality,* Crossroad, 2002). Interiority—a deeper awareness of yourself, your feelings, your values, your needs, your gifts, your family of origin history, your life experience, your story—all of these things. The more you know, the more you are able to become more integrated. It's a growing sense of responsibility or an emerging sense of agency. Jesus says "No one takes my life from me, I lay it down of my own free will." This is a sense of agency, and it takes a lifetime of discipline.

Creativity—developing passion and a generative sense of spirit. One of my favorite stories about this was told to us by our friend Tom Fox who's the publisher of the *National Catholic Reporter.* Tom tells this wonderful story of his daughter Catherine, who's now in her twenties. Tom is married to a Vietnamese woman so their children are Asian-American. Catherine was the first Asian-American woman, I believe, to receive an Olympic gold medal in swimming. She was on the relay team when the Olympics were in Atlanta—we saw her on TV swim to a gold medal. Tom tells us that Catherine was born loving the water. One day they had gone to the abbey at Gethsemani. Catherine was about five years old and she didn't particularly want to be on this trip; it was in the summertime and she wanted to be swimming. As soon as they got there, the head monk came out to welcome them. Catherine rolled the window of the car down and she looked out with her little eyes and said to the monk, "Does Gethsemani have a swimming pool?" The monk said, "No, honey, I'm sorry we don't have a swimming pool." She looked at her dad and she said with all the determination of a five-year-old, "Gethsemani sucks." Catherine's passion was swimming. Imagine the time and the discipline that it took her to go from that five-year-old girl just wanting to splash in a swimming pool to winning a gold medal. Imagine how much time and attention and discipline and passion human love takes. It requires that we reach into the depths of our creativity and give it everything we've got, like Catherine.

Finally, intimacy—another sign that we are moving toward integration. Intimacy doesn't mean necessarily that we're in a love relationship that's happy and wonderful, because we all know that relationships change, people die, things end. Intimacy means that we are working hard at increasing our capacity for self-disclosure, of being an adult who can say like the child, You can see me because I've found the words and the skills to share who I am and I want to see you just as much.

John

If we are to accomplish this great task not only of personal integration but, finally, of communal integration—we're not only individuals, we're part of a church community that's going through an incredible breakdown—how can we re-imagine that we might reclaim the affirming, profoundly positive vision of sexuality as graced and wonderful and responsible? How can we reaffirm this? When people in the church say, What can the church do now to heal? we like to say that the hierarchical church first needs to start listening to the people of God, listen to the stories of loving, love all the stories of loving.

Remember June 2002; in the midst of all the crises the cardinals went to Rome to see the Holy Father. I remember I was standing in line at the grocery store the day they came back from Rome (this was before the meeting in Dallas); there was a picture of all the cardinals on the front page of several of the papers. The woman in front of me was about my age and we were looking at the headlines together. She looked at me and she said, "Pretty sad, isn't it?" And I said "Yeah." And then she said, "Well, I don't know about you, but I'm a Catholic, and I'm a grandmother and I have five children and seventeen grandchildren." And she said, "Help me with this now. These grown men, these cardinals, went thousands of miles across the Atlantic ocean to visit the pope to find out that sexual abuse is a sin and a crime. I could have told them that."

Duh! There is that part of us that goes "Duh!" isn't there? And "Duh!" I don't mean this to be at all facetious, but we won't fully understand this unless we listen to parents, unless we come to understand the safety issues, the vulnerability of children, unless we come to listen to all the love stories of single persons—single persons are sometimes the most neglected group of people in the church because we assume mom, dad, 2.1 kids, and Fido—what about all the other people who are still looking for love, wondering, like Kelly, the young student Fran quoted at the beginning of this chapter, "Is there going to be anybody there to love me and will I find anybody to love?" What about the persons who feel they are in the minority, in the margins? What about our gay and lesbian brothers and sisters? What place do they have at the table of love in our community? So to re-imagine and reclaim the first step we say, "Listen and listen deeply to the stories of other people." To do this is to involve ourselves in yet another important area; we are going to have to rediscover the deep connection between sexuality and justice. Sex and power—this is an intrinsic issue.

The basic sexual sin is not that sex is pleasurable. The basic sexual sin is when it is a violation of persons or commitments. This is what makes it morally wrong. It is not that a body responds as a body was created to be, but that it responds in the wrong context—abusing someone, exploiting someone, using someone, breaking commitments. The church needs to name this. We tend so often to see sexual issues as private issues. We don't see the relational dimensions that are there, that are so profound, that are built in. This is a neglected ethical dimension that will be the future of our healing and the future of our imagination, and it involves a profound prophetic vision.

Back to the prophets. I'll give you one brief, familiar example from the Book of Micah (6:8). The setting is that the people of God have wandered into legalism, moralism, and ritualism. God puts them on trial and brings the mountains in as witnesses against the people. Micah is the prosecuting attorney and he's holding the people accountable. Basically, the people go to Micah and say, "Well let's make an out-of-court settlement. What does God need? Does God need more barrels of oil, more sacrifices, more external ritual?" This is the famous response that Micah gives to the people: "You already know, oh people, what God wants of you, this and only this. To act justly, to love tenderly, and to walk humbly." These three things are profoundly linked. They're not three separate things; they're part of the same stance of the heart—this is the prophetic vision. Justice is God's passionate desire to stand at the side of the little ones. What's missing in the church today—and this is the tragedy—is that the very mission of the church is to be there for the vulnerable. This is our broken wound. We are not there sometimes for the most vulnerable in our community.

I read the book and then saw the film *The Color Purple*. Celie, the main character in that story, was abused in every way a young woman can be abused, physically, emotionally, sexually. Remember the scene at the Thanksgiving dinner: Shug is there, her mentor, and the family is there. Mister is there, who is her abuser. It's time to carve the turkey and Celie stands up with the knife, looks at everybody, and with a fiery passion says, "I may be poor and I may be a woman and I may be black, but I'm here." She was holding the carving knife and for a moment no one knew what she was going to do with it, but she plunged the knife into the carving board. It's her statement. Whoever, whatever your background, however wounded you are, whatever statements you should fill in there for Celie, the most important one in the prophetic vision is "I am here and I am a beloved daughter of God; I am a beloved son of God." This is the call, to recognize that the real sin is the violation of persons. The relationship between sex and power needs to be more profoundly explored.

The relationships between power and systems need to be explored. I remember in 1984, when I was still a pastor, the ABC television network aired the miniseries *Thornbirds*. It was based on a very good novel written by Colleen McCullough.

Priests in many dioceses stood up and said to the people on Sunday, "Don't watch *Thornbirds.*" The people, of course, said, "Well, when is it on?" The reason priests gave for not watching *Thornbirds* was because it's the story of the illicit sexual affair between Father Ralph and the young woman Meggie. Of course, the ABC network was saying to watch *Thornbirds* for the same reason.

Now I had read the book but I never did get to see the miniseries because we had communal penance services every night. It's a very good book for Holy Week. The subplot may be about Meggie and Ralph and their illicit love affair but the story of *Thornbirds* is about claiming, controlling, and climbing. It's about power and the violation of persons. It's about a man who will climb over anybody to get to the top, including the one woman who could have redeemed his life. I didn't hear any bishops or any church people at the time say, "Don't watch *Thornbirds* because you'll be scandalized by the misuse of power." We're used to power and its misuses in the system. What we're talking about here is very profound— naming the misuse of power within systems of secrecy and denial.

In conclusion, a word about the real sexual revolution. In the late fifties and early sixties, when I was a student at the Catholic University of America, going to the seminary, the so-called sexual revolution began to take place. I was just coming into young adulthood at the time. In 1984, *Time* magazine wrote in its cover story that the revolution was over. It's interesting that in that issue of *Time* AIDS is not mentioned once. All the other sexually transmitted diseases are, even though AIDS was already a pandemic at the time. The article said the revolution was over now because of the fear that love could literally kill you. We want to say, and we think you'll resonate with us, that the sexual revolution is not over. On some levels it has not yet truly begun.

The real sexual revolution still lies ahead of us. It still lies ahead of us in these words written fifty years before 1984. At the end of an essay entitled "The Evolution of Chastity," in 1934, Teilhard de Chardin wrote these words. We would like to end with them, and we invite you to claim them as your own, claim them as we have claimed them: "Someday, after we have mastered the winds, the tides, and gravity, we will harness for God the energies of love and then for the second time in the history of the world we will have discovered fire."

For Reflection

❖ How has sexuality been a gift in your own life? How have the loving relationships in your life led you closer to Christ?

❖ How does your parish help people live their sexual lives well? How does it lead people to greater holiness and great love?

❖ Sex is everywhere in the culture around us. How does your parish address a healthy, holy sexuality in the midst of so much sexual misuse in the culture?

Imagine a New Church, Indeed!

I SOMETIMES SIT IN A QUIET CHURCH
>   allowing my eye to follow the light
>   as it streams in through the windows.
There are the smells of burned incense
>   and candle wax
>   and the slightly sour smell of old wine
>   in the air.
And sitting there,
>   I try to imagine what the Church would be like
>   if everyone, *everyone,* was truly welcome there.
Sometimes the lines of that hymn come to mind,
>   the one where we sing and pray
>   that all might be welcome
>   within the church.

Marty Haugen wrote this hymn. It tells a great truth.
It envisions the church as a house
where love can dwell
and where everyone can find
a safe home.
It envisions the church as a place
where prophets can speak
where the truth is told,
and where all the people of God
can dream of God's Reign.
Sometimes I find myself humming this great hymn
while out walking in the fields around our farm,
or driving into the city.
It goes on to dream of a place
where the outcast and the stranger
bear the image of God's face.
The hymn speaks of the church
as that place
where all are truly welcome.

When I wrote
my little book on whole community catechesis,
this song was playing in the back of my mind often.
You can easily see the connection
for how can we ever succeed in catechesis,
or in pastoral care,
or in renewing the world,
or in touching people's lives
if all are not welcome?

I was humming it again during the last Easter season.

Because we worship so frequently
during the Triduum and early Easter Season,
the many readings and stories from Sacred Scripture

tend to swim together in our minds
    and imaginations.
Even if you don't come to church for those days,
    you still know what's going on there:
On Holy Thursday:
    the Last Supper,
    washing of the feet,
    the bringing into each church the oils
        blessed by the bishop
        and used for anointing and baptisms.
On Good Friday:
    the crucifixion and death
    with the reading of the passion story,
    the veneration of the cross.
And then on the holiest night of the year, Holy Saturday:
    the Easter Vigil:
    the candlelight opening,
    the reading of our shared story of salvation,
    the blessing of the fire and the water,
    baptism and confirmation:
        new members initiated into the church community.
Easter Sunday morning:
    lilies,
    fresh water,
    big crowds,
    pink and yellow spring dresses,
    new life,
    a new beginning,
    a strong sense of optimism.
        Alleluias are sung again!

There are two events in this whole story
    that swim together for me.

The first is on Holy Thursday evening
    at the supper meal.
        What strikes me
        is that Jesus was the host there.
            It was his table,
            set for him.
And the second is the moment in which
    Jesus met his disciples in the upper room
    with Thomas doubting it all,
        hidden there behind their locked doors,
        huddled together.
    What struck me in the latter story
        was how Jesus still claimed them as his own!

I mean, these people had,
    for the most part,
    run out on him in his hour of need.
They were full of doubts.
    But to Jesus,
    it didn't matter who they were.
Forgiveness was such a strong theme
    of his teaching and of his practice
    that none of that mattered.
He would still eat with them
    and still invite them to the banquet:
        that fish fry on the beach in John's gospel,
        at Emmaus in Luke's gospel,
        after the supper, in the upper room:
            Let's get something to eat.
In these stories, Christ is the host.
    Christ sets the table.
    Christ welcomes them all!
In thinking about all this,
    I suddenly realized that that's the Good News!

Forgiveness, absolute and total forgiveness,
    was not just one theme among many
    in the gospels.
It was the MO, the Mode of Operating
    for Jesus Christ.

So imagine a Church where we understand
    that in Christ, all are forgiven.
Imagine a Church where we understand
    that the table around which we gather
    does not "belong" to us.
        It is not set by us.
        We don't own it.
        It belongs to Christ.
If we were the ones making up the guest list
    and setting out the meal,
    I suspect it would be less inclusive
        than Jesus' guest list.
Our meal would be a little more skimpy.
    We tend not to forgive as easily,
    and to hold sins against one another.
        We tend to exclude at our tables.

But the good news is that Jesus does not.

The MO here is Christ's, not ours:
    forgiveness is in;
    holding sins against each other is out.

So imagine with me if you will,
    what it would be like
    if we truly meant what that great hymn says
        that *all are welcome.*

Imagine making an announcement before Mass
    next Sunday in your own home parish,
    welcoming all,
        from the crossroads and byways,
        from the darkest corners of society,
        from the forsaken and forgotten and rejected,
        from the outsiders,
            the strangers,
            and the foreigners.
Imagine a stream of people coming into the future Church,
    led triumphantly through the doors
    by—who else?—*by us! The Church's leaders!*

"Who are you?" we might ask,
    "Are you married with kids,
        worrying for them
        and committed to their welfare?
    Are you divorced?
    Are you married for the second,
        or even the third time?
    Are you a single parent
        struggling to make ends meet,
        but also hoping to have love
            in your life again?
    Are you gay or lesbian?
Well if you are, then you belong to us
    because you belong to Christ.
Christ is the host here today and Christ welcomes all!

Who are you?
    Are you lonely?
    Are you a widow?
    Are you a single man or woman
        who would prefer to have a spouse?

Are you disabled or disfigured?
Have you run out of luck?
Does your life seem flat?
Is your faith on a slowdown?
Well if you are, then you belong to us
    because you belong to Christ.
Christ is the host here today and Christ welcomes all!

Who are you?
    Are you struggling financially?
    Have you been laid off?
        Downsized?
    Does it seem like you can never quite get it all
        together?
Well if you are, then you belong to us
    because you belong to Christ.
Christ is the host here today and Christ welcomes all!

Who are you?
    Are you struggling with family planning questions?
    Have you been a victim of abuse or violence,
        of a crime?
    Are you fearful?
    Are you a criminal or imprisoned?
    Do you have a past about which you feel shame?
    Are you homeless or hopeless?
Well if you are, then you belong to us
    because you belong to Christ.
Christ is the host here today and Christ welcomes all!

Who are you?
    Are you new here?
    An immigrant maybe?
    Are you from another religious tradition?

Are you full of doubt today, like Thomas?
Are you fearful like the disciples were?
Has it been a while since you darkened
    the doorway of this church?
None of that matters.
You belong to us *because you belong to Christ*.
Christ is the host here today and Christ welcomes all!

All people of good will are welcome here:
    That's the really good news!
If you've been away,
    you can come back,
    if you've been living in darkness,
        you can come to the light,
    if you haven't been able to believe without seeing him,
        look around you,
        the Body of Christ has come to Mass today.
Sinners are welcome,
    saints, too.
Everyone is welcome to come to Christ:
Our Lord and Our God, indeed!"

Imagine the Church as a beacon on a hill
    beckoning all to come,
    calling all to be here,
        here, the place where Grace is shared!

For Reflection

✧ Who are the people whom you keep at a distance? The ones you are most likely to make feel unwelcome around you?

✧ How does your parish make folks feel welcome at the Sunday Assembly? Who do you imagine feels most unwelcome?

✧ What message does your parish send about the love of God to the neighborhood and town where you live? Whom does the parish seem to say God loves most?

— A New Vision of Hope —
from eight experts on the Second Vatican Council

"As we move further into the third millennium, we are called to be a church where power resides in the weak. We are called to be a church that doesn't dread dreaming; a church unafraid to become what it heals; a church that knows death is a path to life; a church that isn't afraid to forgive—or to ask forgiveness; a church that isn't afraid of speaking truth to power."
—*Nathan Mitchell*

Continuing the Journey:
Celebrating 40 Years of Vatican II

This book has the power to change your outlook on life—and especially to change how you view today's church. Whether you were born well before, smack in the middle of, or long after Vatican II, this book offers you a way to jump into the dialogue begun in the church during those heady years. If you have been inspired by Pope John XXIII's vision of hope, you will continue to be inspired by the variety of perspectives this book provides:

Nathan Mitchell	Forty Years Since Vatican II
Maureen Sullivan	I Hope You Dance
Timothy Mullner	The Greatest Story Never Told!
Monika K. Hellwig	Reading the Signs of the Times in Faith
Maurice O'Connell	The Roadmap for the Journey
Bill Huebsch	Deciding on Reform in the Roman Catholic Church
Jacquie Jambor	Sacramental Renewal into the Future
Robert Blair Kaiser	Speak Out for the Sake of the Church

Available through your local bookstore,
at **www.thomasmore.com,** *or call 1-800-264-0368*